CREATING A DRAMA-FREE WORKPLACE

CREATING A DRAMA-FREE WORKPLACE

THE INSIDER'S GUIDE TO MANAGING CONFLICT, INCIVILITY & MISTRUST

ANNA MARAVELAS

This edition first published in 2020 by Career Press, an imprint of Red Wheel/Weiser, LLC
With offices at:
65 Parker Street, Suite 7
Newburyport, MA 01950
www.redwheelweiser.com
www.careerpress.com

Names and places have been changed to protect privacy.

Previously published in 2005 as *How to Reduce Workplace Conflict and Stress* by Career Press, ISBN 978-1-56414-818-6

ISBN: 978-1-63265-157-0
Library of Congress Cataloging-in-Publication Data
available upon request

Cover design by Kathryn Sky-Peck
Cover photograph © Gcpics | *Dreamstime.com*
Interior photos/images by Anna Maravelas
Interior by Gina Schenck
Typeset in Minion Pro

Printed in Canada
MAR
10 9 8 7 6 5 4 3 2 1

To Ben Maravelas Martin and Nancy Olga Jannik
for their love, and fierce devotion to these ideas.

Contents

Introduction

"I've kept your materials in the top drawer of my desk for seven years and three promotions."

—Graham Holden

The behaviors that destroy trust and connectedness are found in every workplace. When toxic behaviors, such as gossip and mean-spirited speculation rise, we can respond in one of three ways. We can join in and add to the downward spiral of negativity, assume change is not possible and ignore the undercurrent of tension, or we can gather up our courage, raise our collective awareness, and move in the opposite direction. This book is testimony to the third choice.

In the process of resolving more than 300 workplace conflicts, I saw time and again that the human longing for respect and dignity is deep and pervasive. Yet I have met thousands of individuals struggling with hostility and mistrust.

We deserve and desire climates of respect, and by reading this book, you will discover why connectedness and trust slips through our fingers, despite our yearnings for relationships grounded in respect and success. You will learn to avoid the common but devastating missteps that 100 percent of my clients have made.

By adopting the strategies in this book you can eliminate workplace drama, boost your career, enhance your health, and increase your well-being. In the stories that follow, you will discover how to transform tension and hostility into connectedness and build relationships that enhance your life and success.

You will see that when we disagree, two disparate reactions, reflective or reflexive, wrestle for our allegiance. The negativity bias of the brain, which is deep-seated and constantly scanning for threat, tilts us toward irritability and annoyance. However, we can become sensitized to this well-intended but troublesome bias, and consciously choose to react with curiosity and concern instead.

I stumbled across the importance of these insights only because I had the privilege of working with relationships on the razor's edge of permanently dissolving, and helping untangle and heal escalated conflicts.

I found the same handful of missteps in every situation, and I was so taken by the significance, yet little known nature, of these seemingly innocent behaviors that I created a seminar to help employees and leaders avoid the common errors that destroy trust. The classes were an immediate hit and have remained so for twenty years. I've turned the essence of our seminars into this script.

This book is broad enough to take in the current landscape of hostility, yet specific enough that you will learn exactly what to do when you face blame, anger, avoidance, and adversarial factions.

Having the ability to convert conflict into connection affects the outcome of every challenge, interaction, and opportunity. Being able to turn irritability into curiosity and concern will enhance your career, relationships, and well-being.

These solutions are compelling answers to universal dilemmas, and you will discover why my clients have often lamented, "Why didn't someone tell me this before?!"

1

Self-Defeating Habits of Otherwise Brilliant People®

"Any intelligent fool can make things bigger, more complex and more violent. It takes a touch of genius, and a lot of courage, to move in the opposite direction."

—Albert Einstein

When goals go awry, the temptation to blame others is a plucky con-artist that insidiously weaves itself into the fabric of our workplaces. Often, with the implicit support of our organizations, "us vs. them" mentalities walk out the front door with our most precious assets: trust, morale, talent, and productivity.

In the following pages, you will find step-by-step strategies for avoiding, or extracting yourself from, conflict-driven drama and hostility in the workplace.

We are painfully aware that positive energy is diminishing in our society and world, and loneliness is on the rise. The workplace is somewhat shielded by societal trends, but it is not immune, and many of us experience a steady erosion of good-natured camaraderie at work. As one client put it, "Relationships aren't what they used to be."

Hostility, stress, and depression are on the rise

Whenever anxiety and stress dominate a society, self-righteous indignation, irritability, and blame beckon with the false promise of relief.

If we fail to stem the tide of disrespect, our collective future is frightening. Imagine a society that becomes more and more dominated by hostility, rage, incivility, and mistrust.

Many individuals are resigned to increased hostility in our world. Perhaps civility and respect is passé, old-fashioned, or a remnant of a more innocent time that we'll never see again. But no reasonable person *wants* this trend to continue.

With skill and courage, we can make our workplaces a haven from, rather than an extension of, escalated conflict, incivility, and disrespect.

If you adopt and practice the strategies in this book, you'll experience a decrease in anger and depression, benefit from better health and resiliency, hone your ability to painlessly resolve tough issues, preserve alliances that are critical to your career and well-being, and create a legacy of achievement, integrity, and respect.

What we will cover falls into three broad categories:

1. The necessity of positive energy at work, including how to:
    - Protect your health and well-being from the corrosive effects of incivility.
    - Lower your stress levels.
    - Create experiences of connectedness, which is an indispensable source of energy at a cellular level.
    - Win the performance and emotional lottery.

2. Insights into the causes and cures of the current hostility dilemma, including:
    - How to build life-long alliances rather than turning hurting, insecure colleagues into adversaries.
    - The benefits of being hard on the problem, soft on the people.
    - When we're most vulnerable to the bright lights of contempt.
    - Why people and personalities are usually *not* the root cause of conflicts and where to focus instead.

3. Specific strategies, including how to:
    - ▹ Transform ugly, toe-to-toe confrontation into a side-by-side search for solutions.
    - ▹ Avoid being drawn into adversarial factions.
    - ▹ Use reciprocity in your favor and turn Cycles of Contempt into Cycles of Courage.
    - ▹ Change the trajectory of blame-based conversations.
    - ▹ Open the dialogue with a 96 percent chance of a positive outcome.

The daily blitz of aggravations and frustrations is part and parcel of modern life. Our lives are so saturated with stress that if we do not consciously decide how to react, our nervous and cranky brains quietly determine who we become, and how we are seen by others.

The price of contempt

Although workplaces do not have a line item for the costs of contempt, the price tag is cold, hard cash. In one of the following chapters, we'll look at a case study in which the principles outlined in this book saved the organization millions of dollars.

When mistrust contaminates interactions between people or departments, collaboration stops, problem-solving becomes biased, information is distorted, conversations become malicious, and speculation slants to the negative. When teams becomes obsessed with building invisible walls, opportunities for improvement and growth are abandoned. Self-oriented behavior becomes the norm. Paranoia replaces passion, cynicism replaces commitment, fear dulls enthusiasm and pride. When being visible is too big of a risk, creativity and innovation suffer. Employees lay low and dig in.

To my knowledge there isn't a comprehensive index of hostility levels by industry, geography, or across time. However, you can review statistics on costs and causes of negativity in society and workplaces by skimming a list of discrete, but related, findings.

Climate change, anxiety, depression, and anger

- The World Negative Experience Index compiled by Gallup and based on 1,000 interviews in 147 countries, tilted more negative in 2017 than in the last decade. The index tracks people's experiences of stress, anger, sadness, physical pain, and worry.
- Two hundred million individuals will be displaced due to climate change by 2050, in essence becoming "ecoimmigrants" (Fritze et al., 2008).
- G. Albrecht coined the term "ecoanxiety" to describe the chronic or acute reaction to climate-related loss of property, community, social ties, identity, and place.
- Worldwide, suicides are ranked as the second leading cause of death among young adults aged fifteen to twenty-nine, with 804,000 suicide deaths occurring worldwide in 2012, according to the 2018 World Health Organization report.
- 54 percent of respondents in forty nations believe climate change is a *very* serious problem, according to a Pew Research Center report published in April of 2016.
- As the world warms, frustration and aggression increases, which results in more anger and violent crimes (Ranson, 2012).

Loss of well-being in the United States

- Twenty-nine percent of Americans believe that an armed rebellion might be necessary in the near future to protect their liberties from government intrusion (Cassino, Jenkins, 2013).
- Nineteen percent of Americans suffer from anxiety disorder, and an estimated 31 percent of US adults experienced an anxiety disorder at some time during their lives according to a 2017 study by the National Institute of Mental Health (US).

- A 2017 Gallup poll found that 67 percent of lower-income Americans personally worry "a great deal" about hunger and homelessness. In middle-income and upper-income families, the figures are an astonishing 47 percent and 37 percent, respectively.
- Forty percent of American families reported that they struggled to meet at least one of their basic needs (health care, housing, utilities, or food) during the last year (Karpman, Zuckerman, and Gonzalez, Urban Institute, 2018).
- Approximately 40 percent of Americans are "perched on the edge" with vast numbers of middle-class Americans saying they would be unable to cover an unexpected $400 expense. Despite fears of idleness, Philip Alston, the author of the UN study, found that only 7 percent of benefits recipients (i.e., Medicaid) are not working. The majority receiving benefits are working full-time jobs, in school, or giving full-time care to others.
- The percent of elderly (aged sixty-five and older) filing for bankruptcy showed a two-fold increase, and an almost five-fold increase in the percent of older people in the bankruptcy system. Of all Americans filing for bankruptcy, older filers rose from 2 percent in 1991 to 12 percent in 2018 (Thorne, Lawless, and Foohey).
- According to a 2018 American Psychiatric Association study, 68 percent of Americans felt "anxious" or "extremely anxious" about "keeping myself or my family safe" and that 39 percent of Americans feel more anxious that they did a year ago.
- In the United States, suicides increased 28 percent between 1999 and 2014 and were the second leading cause of death for young people aged ten and thirty-four in 2016. There were more than twice as many suicides as homicides, according to data from the Centers for Disease Control and Prevention.
- Nearly half of Americans (47 percent) report feeling alone or left out, and 43 percent feel their relationships are not

meaningful and feel isolated from others. Based on interciews with 20,000 US adults, the loneliest Americans are eighteen to twenty-two years old, according to the 2018 "Cigna US Loneliness Index."

- The Southern Poverty Law Center found 954 hate groups operating in the United States, close to an all-time high since they started monitoring nearly thirty years ago, including a 22 percent increase in neo-Nazi groups from the previous year, as reported in their 2017 data.
- Hate crimes in general rose more than 17 percent in 2017, the third straight year that such attacks have increased, according to data released by the FBI. Law enforcement agencies reported it was the biggest increase in more than a decade.
- Road rage involving a firearm doubled between 2014 and 2016, from 214 incidences to 623 according to Trace, a nonprofit news organization (Biette-Timmons).
- Approximately two-thirds of driving fatalities involve aggressive driving (Goodwin et al., 2015, National Highway Traffic Safety Administration).
- More than 78 percent of US drivers admitted to aggressive driving in a 2014 study by AAA. In a survey of more than 2,700 drivers, almost 4 percent exited their vehicles to confront another driver, and 3 percent (57 million in the last year) admitted to bumping or ramming another vehicle on purpose.

Incivility at work

- In a Pan-European opinion poll, 59 percent of respondents report that one of top three workplace stressors was being "subject to unacceptable behaviors such as bullying or harassment" (European Agency for Safety at Work–EU-OSHA, 2013).
- Ninety-eight percent of individuals have reported experiencing rude behavior in 2011, and half said they were treated rudely at least once a week, up from a quarter in 1998.

Eighty percent lost work time worrying about the incident, 66 percent said their performance declined, and 78 percent said their commitment to the organization declined (Porath, and Pearson in *Harvard Business Review*, 2013).

Incivility usually arises not from malice but from ignorance.
—Christine Porath

- The vast majority of workplace bullies are bosses (Workplace Bullying Institute, Williams, 2011).
- The impact of rudeness on performance is astonishing. Medical teams (one physician and two nurses) were given a cognitive task in a simulation of diagnosing a seriously ill infant. Half of the teams were interrupted twice by a rude doctor and half were interrupted but without disrespect. The teams that experienced the two rude interruptions had a 52 percent drop in performance compared to the other teams! The disrespected teams overlooked data that was right in front of them, struggled with comprehension, and accessing their working memory (Riskin et al., *Pediatrics* 2015).

Even the mild incivility common in medical practice can have profound, if not devastating, effects on patient care. . . . Not only does rudeness harm diagnostic and procedural performance of practitioners, it also seems to adversely affect the very collaborative processes that might otherwise allow for teams to compensate for these effects.
—Riskin et al., 2015

- In an experiment to assess the impact of incivility on customers, an employee was treated rudely by another worker. Twenty percent of the potential customers who witnessed the event said they would use the bank's services in the future, compared to 80 percent who had not witnessed the uncomfortable exchange (Porath, MacInnis, and Folkes).

- Both Millennials and Gen Ys (born after 1980) show signs of increased narcissism compared to previous generations. Citing multiple studies of empirical evidence, Twenge found that values have shifted toward extrinsic (fame, image, and money) and away from intrinsic (affiliation and community), which results in less empathy, less concern for others, and less civic engagement (Twenge, 2013).

We used to be friends

Anxiety and incivility is taking a toll. When we listen closely, we hear accounts of workplace conflict in almost any setting, including coffee shops, airports, family gatherings, book clubs, and gyms. These negative experiences spill into our personal lives and can permanently damage our view of human nature.

Tales of lost loyalty, mistrust, and fear occur so frequently that most people believe these negative experiences are inevitable. We become fearful and observant about who's "in," who's "out," who's in the closed-door meeting, and who's going out for drinks after work.

We care deeply about our work, reputations, and status within our teams and groups. Consequently, experiences of simmering conflict and workplace clashes are among the most distressing events of modern life. We have all listened to stories of workplace conflict with the accompanying themes of depression, self-doubt, anger, and despair.

As conflict and fear escalate, our reactions become more counterproductive and more destructive. Negative, blaming reactions are explosive and traumatizing because *no one* wants to be excluded from the group. I am often struck by the anxiety that borders on panic, when individuals sense their reputations, and therefore their inclusion in the group, are at risk. Our drive to belong to a clan, family, or workplace team is a powerful, ancient instinct. Behaviors that appears aggressive and unreasonable are often the anxious attempts of an unskilled person who is struggling to stay in their workplace community, struggling to be heard, and struggling to be included.

Most of us also have our own stories of workplace drama. Superficially, we might tell these stories because we want validation for our point of view. However, at a deeper level, we are grappling with questions about ourselves and human nature.

- We were friends for years, and we trusted each other. What happened?
- If disagreement could destroy our relationship, are all my alliances at risk?
- Should I pull back from other work relationships and become more aloof?
- What's wrong with me? Why couldn't I fix this?

We will explore answers to these questions. And we will look at the triggers of destructive conflict and mistrust, not only to resolve them, but to avoid them as well. By the end of this book, you will know how to keep disagreement from becoming a center-stage drama and fragmenting your team, department, organization, or family.

With hope, desire for connection overrides fear

Individuals are often skeptical that groups can sustain positive energy over time, but the other two options (hostility or disengagement) are so miserable that most clients are conscientious about preserving positive gains. In the 300 conflicts I've worked through, only once did we fail to achieve a resolution that lasted. There is tremendous relief in connection.

When teams have confidence in a conflict resolution process and facilitator, the speed at which emotions shift surprises everyone. Even in highly adversarial settings, when the journey toward resolution begins, employees and leaders join the process with relief. When projects are announced, there is inevitable grousing, but once we start, individuals pitch in. If confidential interviews are the first step, everyone arrives on time and ready to share. If we offer a seminar, everyone not only attends, they also participate and become energized. Leaders and employees are typically gobsmacked over the group's sudden energy and enthusiasm. When teams believe that the process *could* work they pull together, suspend self-oriented behaviors, and arrive at meetings with sleeves rolled up, ready to engage.

In later chapters, you'll learn that the drive to be connected in healthy, productive communities runs deep in our psyches. Anthropologists tell us that cooperation is an ancient practice and critical to adaptation—the cornerstone of life itself. We realize that healthy communities are the only way to achieve goals that none of us can accomplish alone. The motivation to reconcile exists, we need only remove barriers to its unfolding. When we transform negative cultures into climates of respect and appreciation, we win the energy lottery.

Hoodwinked by the bright lights of contempt

Dignified individuals with MBAs, astronomical IQs, and PhDs make the mistake of retreating into contempt. How does this happen?

There's an obvious temptation that accompanies cutting sarcasm and ridicule. The "payoffs" are so much fun. A good zinger draws a crowd and a guffaw. It is aggressive, it is adrenaline, and it is a kick. However, indignation and aggressive reactions are attractive only if we observe the situation for the short-term.

Unfortunately, the negative repercussions of denigrating others (which we will cover in subsequent chapters) are hidden and delayed. However, when we become aware of the invisible costs of contempt we are deeply motivated to sidestep the attraction.

We'll see in later pages that despite our fears, blame and aggression are *not* human nature. Darwin's findings were overwhelmingly focused on the ability of our species to adapt to changing environments, not survival of the fittest. We don't have to roll over and allow negativity to roll over us. We'll see how the tide can be turned.

Discovering the new frontiers of peace is an inside job. . . . It's time to rely on individual responsibility, which comes from being more responsible for your own energies.

—Doc Childre, *Transforming Stress*

Does this material stick?

When I return to a client site for a new project or to conduct another seminar, attendees from previous years proudly lead me to their work areas where materials from the class still hang on their walls.

Individuals are drawn to these techniques because they offer a less aggressive way of handling frustration. Competent reactions resonate with our desires to be appreciated and to appreciate. They appeal to our better nature and confirm that we can make permanent gains in our efficacy. The habits we'll explore help us build tenacious friendships and sweeten the workplace with warmth.

The only thing we have to let go of is the vindictive jolt of energy that comes from blame and self-righteous indignation. It's a small loss compared to the ocean of achievement and positive energy that we can create and embrace.

Three cultures at work

When I arrive for a conflict resolution project, teams are typically in high negative energy. In one executive team the twelve members couldn't make it through a meeting without someone storming out. However, as we worked to resolve the core issues of their anger, their energy dropped. Previously they had been energized by hostility, and now they had nothing holding them together. I realized there is another source of energy that we tap at work: the energy of connection and appreciation.

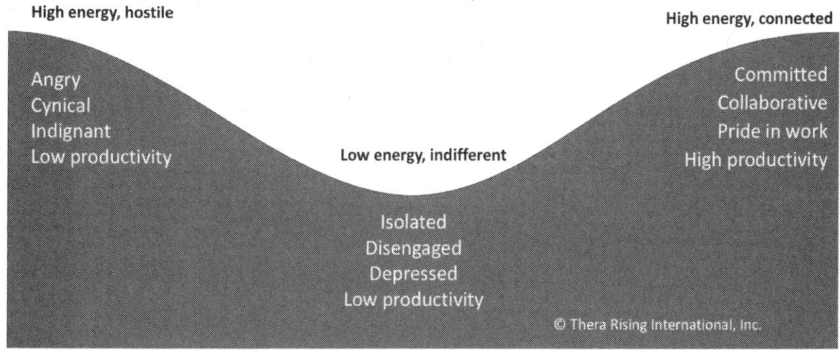

Figure 1.1. Three cultures at work.

I think about these three common workplace cultures—hostile, indifferent, and connected—on a continuum shown in Figure 1.1. On the left are the negative emotions, in the middle is depression and isolation, and on the right end are cultures of commitment and collaboration.

The vertical scale measures the amount of energy these emotions create; energy increases as we move upward. We can see two peaks of energy, at the negative and positive ends, and the loss of energy in middle.

The type of energy in which we live and work has a tremendous bearing on our well-being. Think of different groups to which you belong, such as your current place of work, past jobs, your high school, family gatherings, faith communities, political parties, special interest groups, sports teams, and so on.

You might describe highly negative groups as tense, frightening, irrational, destructive, foolish, wasteful, and tragic. Individuals don't feel safe, they avoid interactions, they skip meetings, and often dread coming to work. Team members experience "Sunday night insomnia." The energy at the left end of the continuum can be dramatic, loud, and manic. High tension is covered up in meetings and explodes later in mean-spirited analysis of another individual's behavior. Anger can be a rush, but feelings of hostility are toxic to our bodies, and incivility and rudeness take a negative toll on performance.

Let's move further to the right on the continuum toward groups that are disengaged. You have probably experienced a job environment with low energy. The culture is dominated by apathy, malaise, or boredom. Solitude and isolation are so uncomfortable that they are used as a punishment in prison. Cultures in the middle of our mental model feel the worst.

One of the most heartbreaking costs of this energy is team members stop thanking and acknowledging each other's contributions. Without this critical feedback, no one knows where they stand or if their efforts are appreciated. In Chapter Three we'll see that without connection, individuals truly suffer.

Employees who work in isolation, or low-stimulus jobs, are especially vulnerable to misbehaving. Employees will do almost anything to escape tedium. This has been borne out in studies of security guards. To avoid a night of mind-numbing boredom, security workers create energy by playing practical jokes, gossiping, and committing minor acts of sabotage.

Anger is toxic to our bodies, but at least we have energy to get out of bed. With indifference (which can gravitate into depression), we feel lousy *and* we lack energy. Consequently, if your team is struggling with escalated conflict we can't simply move away from hostility, reduce tension, and consider the job done. We have to continue our work until team members once again experience the energy of connection. You'll discover that once team members reconnect within a culture of safety and camaraderie, they start to identify solutions that were unattainable just days ago. For many individuals, identifying and implementing solutions is their biggest source of positive workplace energy, hence when achievement diminishes, many employees feel adrift.

Let's move toward good news and the right end of the continuum to cultures based on connectedness and appreciation. Once again energy increases, and we find groups that are pulling together in phenomenal ways. In these cultures, pitching in and going above and beyond one's job description are everyday norms. These environments are productive, fun, energizing, creative, surprising, respectful, and affirming. The atmosphere is loaded with personal and professional advantages. Later, we will explore how this orientation increases effectiveness, prolongs our lives, and decreases our risk for developing deadly diseases. We will also look at data that suggests we are hardwired to connect to each other. We do our best work when we are energized by camaraderie and achievement.

What's the barrier?

If positive energy has so many advantages, why aren't more workplaces driven by camaraderie and trust? My first theory was that the type of energy groups create at work are driven by money. Perhaps groups at the hostile left end of the continuum experience layoffs or budget cuts, and groups at the positive end are successful with no financial worries.

However, my theory didn't pan out. I worked at prestigious law firms that were flush with cash, but had extremely hostile cultures. And I consulted at a small manufacturing company that was laying people off, and they were one of the most bonded groups I'd witnessed in thirty years. I watched as Mikhail, the human resource manager, spoke to the group of employees that were leaving, and tears were running down his face.

He told them this was the worst day of his life. When he finished his presentation several individuals came up to comfort Mikhail and give *him* a hug. Despite their financial hardships, this group was connected!

Clearly it wasn't money that was making the difference. I started wondering if it had something to do with how employees and leaders *respond to frustration.*

Thirty heart hassles a day

In *QR: The Quieting Reflex,* Charles Stroebel, MD, found that we experience an average of thirty "heart hassles" a day. He describes these as moments of "irritating, frustrating, or distressing mini-crises." If you multiple thirty a day by 365 days in a year, that's more than 10,000 a year! Then multiply that number by every employee, leader, client, customer, supplier, and family member. No wonder many of us struggle to feel on top of our game!

Becoming aware of how you react to frustration will change your life because every one of our responses creates positive or negative repercussions (reciprocity) that accumulate throughout our lives.

Frustrations accumulate and amplify

Frustrations can be caused by an acute crisis or the minutia of day-to-day activities. Frustration is a constant, and if we fail to maintain our composure, the residue of each individual annoyance accrues and mounts.

Incidences of frustration are not isolated. A poorly handled frustration in the morning sets us up physiologically for increasingly negative reactions as the day unfolds. When we don't handle aggravations well, it not only makes the next irritation more difficult to manage, but we can become estranged from our personal and professional networks. We lose access to warmth, laughter, joking, light-hearted chatter, compassionate advice, and friendly sounding boards. Life feels lonely and barren.

Having a skill set that allows you to maintain mood and momentum during periods of high stress is a critical life proficiency. Even though frustration is one of the most predictably disruptive aspects of modern life, your ability to manage it is seldom addressed.

Two sources of energy

While at a conference, I stumbled on the work of HeartMath, a nonprofit research organization in Boulder Creek, California, that does research into the physiology of energy. HeartMath uses biofeedback data to understand and manage the energy of emotions. Although our organizations do very different work, we came to the same conclusion: there are two primary sources of energy.

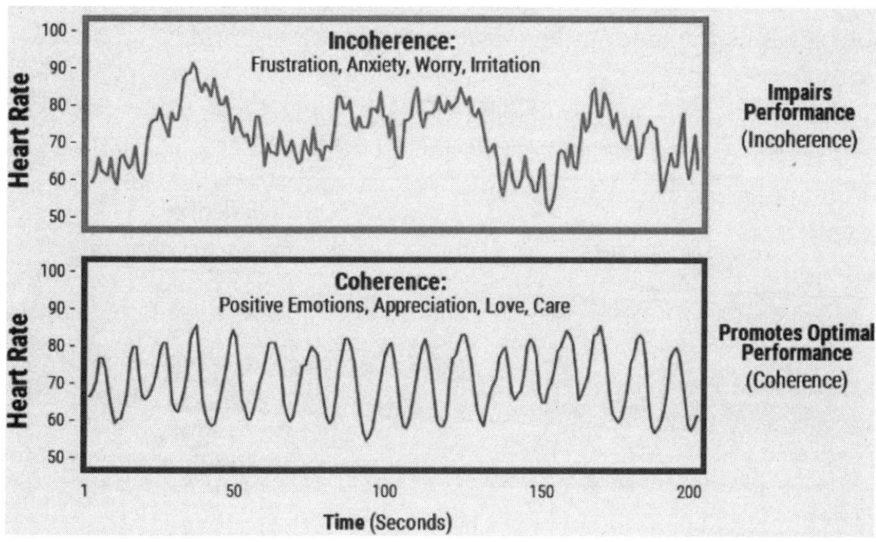

Figure 1.2. Heart-rhythm patterns. Courtesy of HeartMath Institute, ***Heartmath.org*****.**

Figure 1.2 is an electrocardiogram (ECG) of heart frequencies that HeartMath observed while monitoring biofeedback data. In the energy of frustration, there are extreme variations in heart rhythms. The body is working hard, but it is not in sync. HeartMath calls this rhythm "incoherent." It's like a hardworking engine in need of a tune-up.

In contrast, heart variations during periods of connectedness indicate coherence in the body. In this state, the cardiovascular, immune, hormonal, and nervous systems function efficiently. We experience greater mental clarity and creativity. In Chapter Three, we'll discover that our bodies ache for the energy of connectedness.

Assumption, emotion, behavior

Every time we face frustration—the way we think about it, not the event itself—determines our level of irritation and how effectively we respond. Most of us continuously and unconsciously ask ourselves, "What is the barrier to my goal?"

You can see this in the middle column of Figure 1.3, assumptions trigger emotions, which influence how we behave. Becoming aware of this rapid sequence and being able to recalibrate our thoughts and reactions gives us tremendous leverage over how we respond.

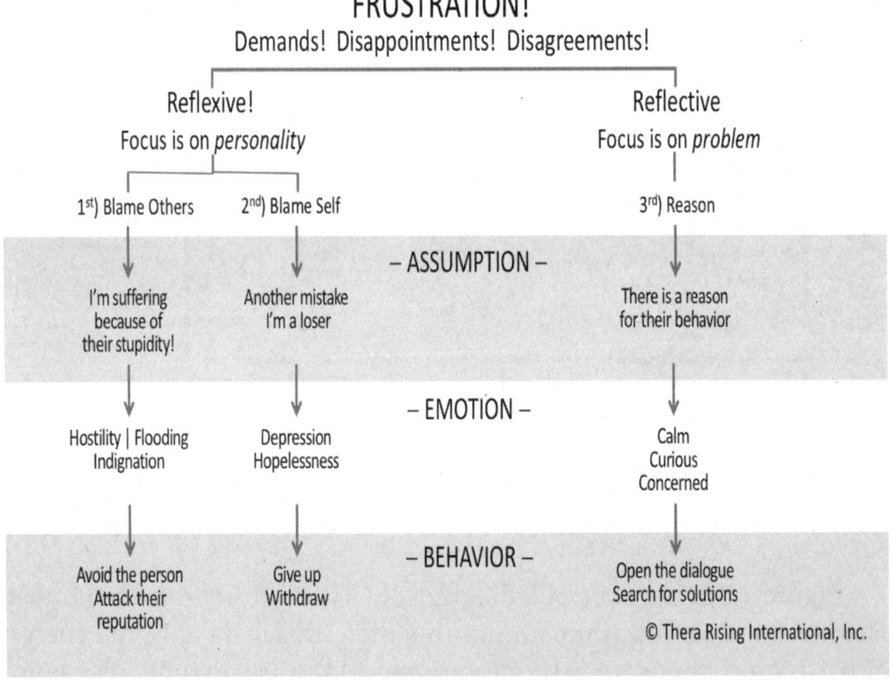

Figure 1.3. Frustration triggers assumptions, emotions, and behaviors.

First, Second, and Third Assumptions

We go down one of three mental pathways when we are frustrated. First Assumption, or blame others, is reflexive and inflammatory, and it targets people and personalities as the source of a problem. This response is a version of "I'm suffering! Who's fault is it?" This assumption results in feelings of indignation. We may start "flooding," which is the bio-feedback word for anger. We'll dive into the physiology of flooding in Chapter Two.

Negative emotions set us up to either attack the person (or group) or avoid them. In the workplace it is often a verbal (not physical) attack and typically it's a criticism of people's competence and character. In the short-term, this reaction triggers a reliable jolt of energy and adrenaline, but it cinches long-term failure, and often we lose the relationship with the person or group we blame. In Chapter Two we'll examine the health risks and consequences of anger.

The other behavior option in First Assumption is avoidance, which is passive and seems like a low-risk behavior. Later, we'll peel this back and see that because work is interdependent, avoidance is a disaster in the workplace.

Second Assumption is a form of harsh self-criticism, and it typically begins to dominate thinking after the adrenaline response fades. This reaction turns the power of contempt inward. This response is similar to, "This is *my* fault! Why didn't I see this coming?!" It might cause us to feel shameful, depressed, and incompetent. We might withdraw or close down. Self-loathing results in the loss of energy and an increase in hopelessness.

In scholarly studies, First and Second Assumptions are called Personality Attribution. We attribute the cause of the problem to people and personalities ("You're a jerk!" or "I'm the loser!"). Although these reactions are widespread and growing in many forms of society, they don't serve us well. Not only are we not able to solve problems in First and Second Assumption, the emotions are debilitating. When we are psychologically aroused it is similar to being in a cognitive fog.

In Chapter Two, we'll explore how First and Second Assumption are linked. The more we blame others, the more likely we are to turn the arrow of contempt on ourselves when we make a mistake.

The pathway that saves our sanity and productivity

Third Assumption, or Situational Attribution, is a reflective, analytical response, and when problems occur, this thinking pattern focuses on situations, not people. This response keeps us calm and makes us curious. Third Assumption is the only mental pathway that primes us to open the dialogue and solve the problem.

In Chapter Three, we'll explore the benefits of this response to our careers and well-being. However, because of the negativity bias of the brain, this response requires awareness, self-reflection, practice, and discipline.

Our thinking is self-fulfilling

Each of these three choices (hostility, disengagement, and connection) are validated by the people around us and our life experiences.

The seeds for these orientations are set in our family of origin. Fortunately, at any age we can seize control of our energy patterns by paying attention to how we *think*. Not only can we heighten our awareness of our choices, we also have built-in mentors; later in the book we'll look at how we can use our *emotions* to get ongoing feedback about the effectiveness of our thinking.

When we get energy from hostility and contempt, blame people for problems, trust only a few select individuals, and view others as adversaries, then our hostile, paranoid feelings and interactions will confirm our beliefs.

Similarly, when we believe that we are essentially alone, that life is meaningless, that effort is unrewarded, that relationships will disappoint, and missed opportunities abound, then our isolation and lack of recognition will confirm our beliefs.

In contrast, when we work hard to build and earn respect, do what it takes to achieve our goals, get a thrill from learning and problem-solving, and reach out to others in times of need, then our social and professional advancements confirm our beliefs.

A senior state agency director who has worked under many different commissioners summarized the differences between these approaches.

> Some of our commissioners come out to the field during a crisis, and their goal is to punish people. They immediately create climates of fear and tension. When these commissioners arrive, everyone scatters.

> Other commissioners seek to understand *how* the problem occurred. They express appreciation for people's efforts and invite staff to join in problem-solving. When they arrive, everyone pitches in to get at the root cause of the difficulty. My direct reports love working for the latter, and hate working for the former.

Outside of work, our worldviews are further reinforced by the kind of entertainment, music, friends, and colleagues to which we gravitate. There are so many opportunities to tap into these different perspectives that we unconsciously begin to narrow where we focus our attention.

Where do you and your team fall on the continuum?

You might wonder which of the three categories you and your team could land: hostile, indifferent, or positive. Groups and individuals move to the left (hostility) and right (positive energy) depending on how stressed, exhausted, relaxed, or threatened they feel. However, most teams have a set point that is a fairly good average.

If it's not immediately obvious where you fall on this continuum as an individual, imagine where you would put your closest friends. It is likely your orientations are similar.

If we scan radio and TV stations, we'll find lots of programs that cater to the reflexive, inflammatory energy of contempt. We also can find programs that provide listeners with a more reflective approach. In these broadcasts, the producers seek to uncover the underlying reasons for world and domestic events. These programs are driven to reveal root causes of social ills, create connections, and propose solutions.

These differences reflect unique thinking patterns that we'll look at closely in the following pages. The impact of these reactions on our effectiveness, relationships, mood, and health cannot be overstated as the following parable illustrates with humor and simplicity.

What do we find in the village ahead?

A traveler, walking along a dusty road, sees an elderly man sitting by the roadside. Abruptly he shouts, "Hey! Old man! What kind of people live in the village ahead?"

The elder asks, "What did you find in the village you just left?"

"Scoundrels," the traveler grumbles, "we drank and gambled, and in the middle of the night I was robbed!"

"Ah," the elder says wisely, "that's what you'll find in the village ahead."

A short time later, another traveler on the same route sees the elderly man.

"Tell me," the second traveler asks kindly, "what kind of people will I find in the village ahead?"

The old man responds with the same question, "What did you find in the village you just left?"

"Oh," responds the traveler, with obvious merriment, "I really enjoyed the people I met! They were intelligent and generous. We told stories about our journeys and shared our simple meals."

"Ah," the elder replied, "That's what you'll find in the village ahead."

The sage understood that we create our realities through subtle, ongoing choices that reinforce our worldviews. These choices lead us to experiences that we unconsciously anticipate, and find again.

Later in this book you'll learn why the negativity bias of the brain tilts us toward fear-based reactions, how to compensate for this tendency, and consciously make choices that optimize your well-being, happiness, and effectiveness. Jackpot!

2

The Stinky Twins: Blaming Others, Blaming Self

"After anger comes shame."
—Benjamin Franklin

I was discussing the physiology of negative energy during a seminar and had just finished a module on "flooding," the biofeedback word for anger. Bruce, an attendee, had been riveted by the discussion. Now we were on break, and he couldn't stop talking.

Bruce told me he was a combat veteran who struggled with reflexive, aggressive reactions to frustration and threat. He said, "I just can't get a handle on my anger, and I've pushed everyone away. Everyone that cared about me has left. I want to tell you, Anna, that I've learned more about anger in the first two hours of your class than I have in twenty years of outpatient therapy at the VA." I simultaneously felt sad that Bruce had struggled for so long without the simple information we covered and relieved that he was learning data he found useful.

A year later, I was back at the same organization, and Bruce sat through the seminar again. "I'm doing so much better! I can't say that I've completely stopped flooding, but it's much less often and it doesn't last as long. I didn't tell you this, Anna, but when I met you, I felt so discouraged and hopeless that I was going to end my life. But sitting in your seminar I realized there is a totally different way to look at the world."

Three years later, we saw each other again. Bruce walked into a seminar and sat in the back. On break he came over and said,

> I've started doing volunteer work! I joined a local service organization, and I got elected president!
>
> During our last meeting, an issue surfaced that has always triggered an argument, and one of the other volunteers flooded. Using the technique you taught us, I was able to calm him down. We went back to discussing the issue and this time, at last, we came to an agreement. Then to my surprise, I realized the energy in the room was at the ceiling—and it was positive!
>
> And then the greatest thing of all happened. I realized *I* could create the positive energy I had waited for other people to bring to me. I'm not afraid anymore! Learning the material in the seminar was the beginning of this shift, and I will never forget it.

Bruce had been on a mission to regain his inherent right to healthy connections and positive feelings about himself and others. He not only developed new skills to control his anger, but he also learned he could dissipate anger in others. With these new competencies, his vitality was restored.

A healthy brain exists to carry out your instructions—you are the composer, it is your instrument.
—Deepak Chopra, MD

The previous chapter covered the three cultures at work and a brief overview of First, Second, and Third Assumptions. In this chapter we will zero in on First and Second Assumptions—the two reflexive responses that had been Bruce's nemeses—blaming others and blaming self. As we'll see, using reflexive assumptions when we are frustrated not only makes us hostile, but as Bruce intimately knew, it makes us more vulnerable to loneliness and depression.

Blaming others when we face one of our thirty frustrations a day is giving our brains the command "Search for stupidity! Whose fault is this?" We assume someone else is causing our frustration: a peer, a boss, a customer or client, another department, or a colleague who snubbed us in yesterday's meeting.

When we search for blame, we focus on people and personalities, such as, "I wouldn't be bringing work home tonight if my boss wasn't such an appeaser—always trying to impress his boss!" Or, "The executive team rejected our proposal because it wasn't their idea and they are control freaks!"

The chilling reality of this approach is that our brains will find data that makes the other person look irrational and unreasonable. Similar to searching for data on Google, once we limit our search to assumptions of blame, our minds will present only the data that fits our search criteria. For a dramatic example of how compliant our brains become once we see someone in a negative light, jump forward to "Transforming the Enemy" in the Epilogue. It's a cautionary tale of how I struggled for seven years with a seemingly insurmountable problem, only to discover that part of the problem lay between my ears.

Negativity bias: Our brains are nervous and cranky!

The body insists we pay attention to threat, but it is relatively nonchalant about positive experiences. In *Hardwiring Happiness,* neuropsychologist Rick Hanson, PhD, reports that negative experiences are five times more powerful than positive events. Hanson labels negative experiences as "Velcro" because of their ability to stick. However, positive experiences more closely resemble Teflon because they slip away without much neurological impact or recall.

Hypervigilance to danger was an evolutionary advantage when sudden death was a constant threat. Subsequently, we remember negative events (or threats) more clearly and intensely.

For a modern-day example of the negativity bias, imagine the last time you were at a family gathering. You probably talked to a number of individuals, but it is likely that after the event, the interactions you ruminated about on the way home were the negative remarks or perceived slights.

In reality, there were probably more positive than negative comments. So why do those little jabs take up more than their share of brainpower?

The answer rests on one small, but often overlooked, evolutionary reality: We can miss many positive events—beautiful sunsets, a good meal, bonding over the campfire. But we can only miss *one* threat.

Consequently, even in our air-bagged and hand-sanitized world, our brains scan constantly for danger—the arched eyebrow of the senior leader, fender-benders on the highway shoulder, or the conversation that stops when we enter the room.

When we avoid others and cut off communication, the negativity bias tilts us toward speculation that is suspicious and self-fulfilling. We will talk more about this in Chapter Four.

Master of First Assumption

For a vivid example of the ineffectiveness of blaming others—especially when facing complex systemic problems—we need look no further than Hitler's Nazi Germany.

Hitler's reign is a classic example of a leader who rose to power on the machinery of dehumanization and contempt. He pitched his ideology to a perfect audience: a disillusioned and suffering population. Germans were not only depressed by years of economic stagnation, they were also bitter about the restitutions imposed by the Allies after World War I. Germany lost land, colonies, and the right to maintain an army, and was saddled with crushing debt. The majority of Germans felt trapped, and hopeless.

Hitler blamed Germany's problems on developmentally and physically disabled children and adults, Catholics, Romani wanderers, gays, lesbians, and the Jewish community. Hitler claimed these sub-groups, who had few advocates, were a drain on the German economy and the cause of its economic crisis. He created a rationale to justify slowly decimating these groups for "the good of Germany."

Despite the fact that Hitler's elimination of these groups had no impact on the economy, Hitler didn't stray from his ideology. His legacy paints a clear picture of the tragedy, futility, and irrationality of targeting *people*.

In Chapter Three, we will look at the same crisis using Third Assumption, which is analytical and situational. While Hitler was busy promoting hatred against minorities, other world leaders were looking for solutions to change the structure of their economic systems, lessening the impact of a lingering drought, and passing laws to shore up unregulated banks.

At many levels, contempt has become a defining characteristic of American politics. . . . This stops the learning process cold and creates a ready-made audience for demagogues . . .
—Madeline Albright, former US Secretary of State and Ambassador to the UN

Today there are many First Assumption leaders. We can identify them by their tendency to label and dehumanize. First Assumption leaders excel at blaming complex, systemic problems on subgroups that are often, but not always, unpopular and vulnerable.

Inflammatory thinking

When people are blamed for problems, frustrations skyrocket. Inflammatory thinking exaggerates the significance and pervasiveness of the inconvenience. When we inflame an event, we use words and phrases such as, "Always," "Never," and "They're all alike."

- I can't stand this! Why is the copier always out of paper?
- Just my luck! My computer is down, and now I'll never get this report out!
- Everyone in marketing is a slacker!

In this chapter, I introduce situations in which reflexive assumptions, blame, and inflammatory thinking took center stage. We will return to these stories in the next chapter to see how outcomes changed dramatically when individuals shifted their thinking to Third Assumption.

Fear triggers a tsunami of blame

Tony enjoyed many years as an attorney in a sophisticated manufacturing company. Being the conscientious employee that he was, he arrived early for the all-staff meeting at which the company president was scheduled to give an update on acquiring a new facility.

However, once staff had settled, they were stunned to learn that instead of purchasing a local building, the president was closing the existing office and moving the organization to his hometown halfway across the country.

The owner's reasons for the sudden change were vague. He tried to reassure the employees by saying the "brightest and best" would be invited to relocate. Undeniably, the rest of the workforce would soon be without jobs. Tony's colleagues walked back to their departments in shock. Within a few minutes, their surprise turned to outrage and blame.

Tony had worked across the organization and had developed friendships in every department. Consequently, he spent the next hour walking through the facility listening to his colleagues vent. The engineers turned against their traditional foe: "This is marketing's fault! They dropped the ball on customer feedback and trends."

Tony wandered into the next division and heard equally angry reactions in the sales group: "I told the engineering department to back down! But they didn't listen. They kept adding features to our products that drove our costs sky-high. South Korea and Japan didn't help either! They've bulldozed their way into the American market!"

Tony wandered back to the legal department and saw the attorneys huddled in a circle with their own ideas about who was to blame: "The owner is probably returning to his home state so he can hunt and fish! He's your typical egocentric executive, thinking only of himself and *his* retirement! To hell with us!" In the next chapter, we will see how inaccurate these speculations were.

Predictable workplace targets and scapegoats

When the thinking patterns of blame and contempt take over an organization, no one is safe. Individuals or entire groups are targeted for any conceivable reason. Frontline workers blame the boss; the CEO blames the board; second shift blames first shift; the COO blames the plant in Taiwan; architects blame project managers; Millennials blame Baby Boomers; the city council blames the mayor; support staff blames administration; firefighters blame headquarters; and branch offices blame corporate.

I've watched many leaders foolishly attempt to create team cohesiveness through hostility and denigration of other people or departments with statements such as, "Those jerks in sales don't care if we make a profit off this order!" For groups, hostility and blame are used as the "sugar high." It is quick and easy because channeling anger toward a convenient target takes little effort or skill.

The more frequently we entertain anger, the more we reinforce specific neural pathways in our brains. With enough repetitions, the blame response becomes automatic and less conscious.

Anger, hostility, impaired immune systems, and heart disease

Blaming others sidesteps the nitty-gritty work of problem-solving, and it helps generate a burst of energy when the team is in a slump. However, one of the many costs of hostility and blame is a dramatic increase in the risk for heart disease.

Researchers call anger "flooding" because our bodies "flood" with cortisol and adrenaline. As thinking inflames, so do our bodies.

Dr. Redford Williams, a psychiatrist and director of the Behavioral Medical Research Center at Duke University, suspected that hostility was the biggest predictor of heart disease. Dr. Williams found twenty-five-year-old personality tests (the MMPI) that were given to law students. One of the traits measured by the test is the individual's hostility level. Williams suspected that if his hypothesis were correct, he would find a correlation between high levels of hostility and early death rates.

Williams found that in the low-hostility group, 5 percent had died during the following twenty-five years. However, 20 percent of the high-hostility group had died from various causes, but primarily from heart disease. In his bestselling book *The Trusting Heart,* Williams concluded that frequent, prolonged, and intense anger is the best predictor of death rates from coronary blockage.

Our defense system secretes chemicals to thicken our blood so we don't bleed out if we are physically wounded. As a result, people who are fueled by a regular diet of hostility can be quietly developing arteriosclerosis, or hardening of the arteries, in response to elevated levels of blood-thickening chemicals.

When we become angry, our bodies rapidly increase the amount of available energy through an increase in hormones, blood pressure, and pulse rate. Cortisol, one of the hormones released during heightened anger, is a particularly troublesome chemical. It damages the cells lining the heart and makes it more difficult for the body to maintain equilibrium.

This process is controlled by an ancient defense system designed to ensure you can outrun a hungry predator. However, in today's culture, individuals can have elevated levels of cortisol and adrenaline in reaction to the inability to manage relatively minor emotional events. The majority of modern-day risks for heart disease are not created by the threat of physical danger; they are created by our reactions to emotional risks.

Under the influence of First Assumption and inflammatory thinking, we assume the solution is outside our control. We can't solve the problem unless *they* change, and consequently, we feel trapped! Our bodies react with aggression and fight-or-flight. Blame can turn a minor inconvenience into a perception that this is not only an injustice, it is also intolerable. Once we flood, it takes a *minimum* of two hours for the chemicals to leave our bloodstream. Each frustration adds to the chemical overload of the previous incident. This data helps us understand why, once we flood, the rest of our day can easily deteriorate.

No matter how many times you work out at the gym or how careful you are to eat correctly, you're putting yourself at risk if you don't manage your anger effectively.

—Hendrie Weisinger, PhD

In *The HeartMath Solution,* Doc Childre and Howard Martin present evidence that even five minutes of *recalled* anger impairs the immune system for six hours!

At 100 heartbeats per minute, we can't hear

Researcher and psychologist John Gottman PhD, spent twenty years obtaining biofeedback data (heart rhythms, blood pressure, etc.) on couples while they were engaged in tense discussions. In his book *The Seven Principles That Make Marriages Work,* Gottman relates that the human body will go from a normal heartbeat (eighty-two beats per minute for women and seventy-six for men) to 165 beats per minute when we feel threatened. "When we wire up couples during a tense discussion, you can see how physically distressing flooding is." Gottman concludes that it's almost impossible to have rational thoughts when we are flooded.

Gottman found that when we're flooded and our heartbeats go above 100 beats per minute, blood pressure interferes and we cannot hear what the other person is saying, even if we try.

I wonder if this biological reality plays a factor in police shootings. In July of 2016, not far from where I live, Philando Castile, a school aid and a well-loved member of the community, was killed when he was pulled over by the local police.

In the police dashcam video, Philando says, "Sir, I have to tell you that I do have a firearm on me," and the officer screams, "Don't reach for it!" before he fires seven times, fatally shooting Castile.

When I watched the video, Officer Jeronimo Yanez is clearly flooded. Even though Castile seems calm in the tape, I'm sure his heart was beating more than 100 beats per minute. Although many factors contribute to these tragedies, what if neither person had been able to hear? The officer sees Philando doing exactly what he is telling him *not* to do, and Philando can't hear that his actions to save himself are going to contribute to his death. Perhaps understanding and managing the physiology of flooding can help us walk back from these tragic events.

Men rage, and rescue

Our species was organized in small clans of hunters and gatherers for 99.99 percent of the time we have been on the planet. Men and women relied on, and respected, the contributions of the other gender, but we were bound by rigid gender roles: women gathered and men hunted. These differences are still reflected in our physiology.

Our remarkable technological accomplishments notwithstanding, modern human beings still occupy cavemen bodies.
—Charles Stroebel, MD

As hunters, men faced many dangers. The ability to flood rapidly and intensely was a necessity to fend off physical danger and to subdue prey. Men were aggressive hunters and they were protectors of women and children.

These ancient differences help us understand why 96 percent of the people in prison for violent crimes are males.

However, this increased ability to flood also contributes to men performing a higher percentage of rescue work. When it comes to physical attributes, flooding boosts speed and strength. Consequently, if your life is at risk, flood!

Emotional idiocy

When we flood, problem-solving, which occurs in the cortex, the largest and most analytical part of the human brain, is impaired. As a result, we can't think of a pointed response when we're in a heated argument. To add insult to injury, when the point you were trying to make pops up fifteen minutes later, we think, "Why didn't I say . . .?" This is a good example of the amygdala at work, hijacking higher systems of thought.

The amygdala, which is the size of a *walnut,* lies at the base of the skull and is the most active part of the brain when we are flooded. It's easy to understand why people behave in ways that make no sense when they are angry: sports fans that throw garbage on the field because their team is losing, parents who attack the youth referee because they disagree with a call, or the boss who loses his cool in a meeting and (in the words of Laurence Peter) "Makes the best speech he'll ever regret."

Walnut brain

There are two primary reasons I focused on the causes, costs, and antidotes of anger in my work. One is to help many clients and teams that were struggling with flooding.

The other reason is more personal. My father was a combat Marine veteran who never received help for his flooding and subsequent violence. His uncontrolled rage, often targeted at his children, became one of the defining forces in our lives. My parents had six children, and we all have different memories of my dad's anger. Many years into adulthood I asked a very kind woman, who had been our next door neighbor, what she remembered. Her answer confirmed my experience. She said, "When your dad got angry, I would bring my children into the house."

As unbelievable as it seems today, in the days when my father terrorized us with his rage, the police weren't called; it was considered a domestic problem for the family to handle. Consequently, my primary emotional reactions were fear and shame. Shame that we could not stop him, shame that the neighbors knew. Finally, in my twenties, I confronted my father and told him that if he ever hurt one of us again, I would call the police.

Here is the irony of flooding: My father didn't know what I was talking about. At first I thought he was in denial, or maybe this conversation was too much for him. But later I learned another possible cause for his confusion: memory is impaired when we flood. Once I understood this, I started seeing examples of this phenomena in the media. A person arrested for a violent crime says something similar to, "I remember we were yelling, then my memory goes blank, and the next thing I can recall is the police at the door."

I have seen this in the workplace also. A university professor in a struggling department flooded frequently and intensely. She confided, "I don't remember what happens after I get angry. I have one friend in the department, and he'll fill me in the next day." If the purpose of flooding is speed and strength at the expense of IQ, then faulty memory makes sense.

Ironically, but not surprisingly, as much as I witnessed the damage of my father's fury, I adopted his habits and became a flooder myself. Although I never physically attacked anyone, I internalized his behavior and believed it was appropriate to rant, rave, and slam doors.

Once I was furious with a friend who repeatedly promised to bring a chair for my home office. When he finally delivered on his promise, it was dreadful. The fabric was torn, stuffing was coming out, and it was missing a wheel, making it lopsided. I was so angry over his delays and false promises that I opened a second-story window and threw out the chair!

I tell the story about the chair in seminars because I want attendees to know that I *get* how insidious, shameful, and habitual anger can become. Also, people in the seminars are usually shocked because today I could be an advertisement for calm behavior, which gives individuals hope that they can get on top of their flooding too.

In Chapter Seven, we'll cover the techniques I used to stop flooding, but I want to share one of my favorites in this chapter. After I learned about the role of the tiny amygdala in flooding, I used it to my advantage. I hate being stupid, which is essentially what flooding does to us all. So, when I was tempted to flood, I'd think, "Walnut brain, walnut brain." Just the thought that I would both lose my capacity to solve the problem and potentially harm a relationship motivated me to control my anger.

Intelligence capacity is diminished when frustration, anxiety, or inner turmoil operate. Such emotional states cause incoherence in the rhythmic and electrical output of the heart, diminishing neurological efficiency. It's one of the reasons smart people can do stupid things.

—Doc Childre and Bruce Cryer

A fire chief gave me an additional insight. Flooding is a serious concern in his line of work. It's the job of the chief to analyze the best way to approach a fire, a job that requires years of experience and training. When the chief looks at a burning building, the images are so visceral that they activate the fight-or-flight response. As a result, in most situations, the chief stands so his or her view of the fire is blocked, and the only information they receive is auditory.

Venting

Therapists used to encourage people to act out their aggression in order to release anger. Individuals with suppressed rage were encouraged to beat on pillows with plastic bats as a means of resolution and release.

However, research done at Iowa State University by Dr. Brad Bushman concluded that venting doesn't eliminate or dampen the expression of violence; it makes it more likely that it will occur again. Dr. Bushman wrote, "Venting to reduce anger is like using gasoline to put out a fire—it only feeds the flame. By fueling aggressive thoughts and feelings, venting increases aggressive responses."

Venting weakens our natural inhibitions against violent outbursts and, according to HeartMath, reinforces the neurons that make this reaction automatic. In her book *Anger: The Misunderstood Emotion*, author Carol Tavris wrote, "The biggest, fattest cultural myth, the elephant in our living room . . . is that catharsis is good for you."

Yelling

During a seminar, a construction supervisor named John blurted out, "But you don't understand; yelling at people works! When I yell at a contractor, I get results. They move!" I felt empathic to his frustration because I was challenging one of his favorite motivational strategies. John's employees were moving, but their ability to problem solve was impaired. When supervisors flood and scream at site operators, the operators scramble, but they will be unable to think analytically.

In addition, the recipient will be focused on revenge. If John rants at employees, he'll never discover how the employee saves face with his or her peers, be it a cutting retort behind John's back or an act of sabotage at the construction site. In later chapters we'll explore retribution, retaliation, and revenge in detail.

First Assumption: I'm frustrated and it's your fault!

Let's take a look at the flow between inflammatory thinking, flooding, and behavior through the following true story.

A driver focuses her attention on the back seat while she's at a red light. Sure enough, when the light changes, she doesn't notice. The male behind her taps his horn impatiently, but she ignores him. The female driver gets out of her car, opens the back door, and starts digging around in the back seat! The driver behind her leans on his horn, rolls down his window, and screams at her to get out of the way. She continues to ignore him, but within a minute or two, she returns to her seat and drives away.

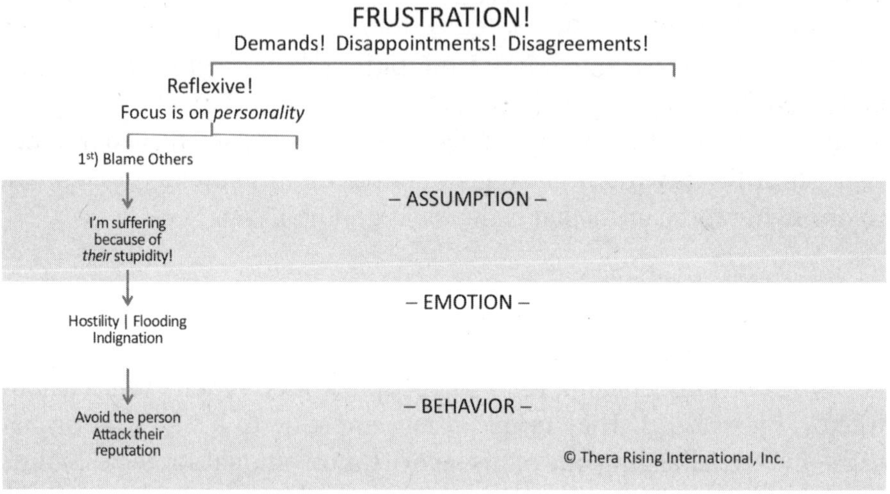

Figure 2.1. First Assumption, blame others.

If we generate examples of blaming, inflammatory responses to this situation, they might include:

- "She's oblivious. Stupid Millennial!"
- "She's an old lady with nothing better to do."
- "Woman driver! She's putting on her makeup."
- "She's filthy rich and doesn't care about anyone but herself."
- "She's unemployed and has nowhere to go."
- "She's too stupid to realize the light has changed."
- "She's an immigrant, and none of them care about our rules!"

When individuals are asked to brainstorm examples of blame in response to this story, the energy in the room skyrockets. People are laughing and boisterous. The energy of blame is self-righteous and indignant. But if you analyze the list of reactions, you'll notice that all of these statements are assumptions about the driver and her character. She is attacked for being stupid and for her personality, gender, economic status (too poor or too rich), age (too young or too old), and ethnicity.

As you know, with inflammatory thinking we feel hopeless about finding a solution, so the frustration seems insurmountable and unmerited. *It's this approach to solving the problem that causes us to flood, not the problem itself.*

Second Assumption: I'm frustrated and it's my fault

Sometimes instead of blaming others, we turn contempt inward and blame ourselves. This reaction is less visible. Most of us blame others publicly, but berate ourselves privately. Depression comes from the same thinking pattern as hostility toward others—the arrow of blame just swings inward.

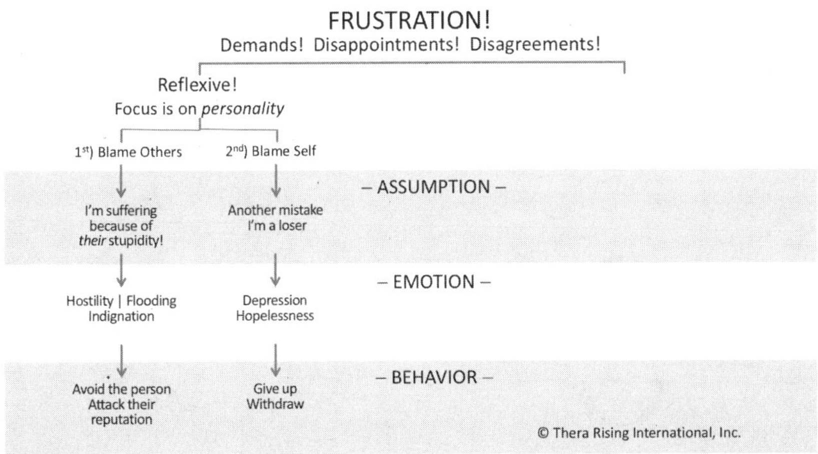

Figure 2.2. Second Assumption, blame self.

If we're stuck behind someone who behaves in a seemingly irrational manner, we might initially react reflexively with First Assumption and blame.

However, when the adrenaline and cortisol fade, blaming and shaming voices turn on us. In Second Assumption, responses sound like: "Boy, I really lost it back there. I'm such a mindless jerk for getting angry over something so minor. I was in such a huge hurry, but my client was delayed and didn't even realize I was late. I'm such a loser."

Some individuals resort to self-contempt immediately upon becoming frustrated. While checking out at the grocery store we can really damage our sense of well being when we inflame our thinking with "I *always* pick the wrong line!"

Depression, work, and health

Like hostility, depression has negative effects on health and productivity. A study by Geisinger Health Systems found that approximately 9 percent of the workforce is affected by depression at any given time, but it is often invisible to bosses and coworkers. Depressed employees report losing more than five hours per week from reduced performance due to fatigue, irritability, and loss of focus.

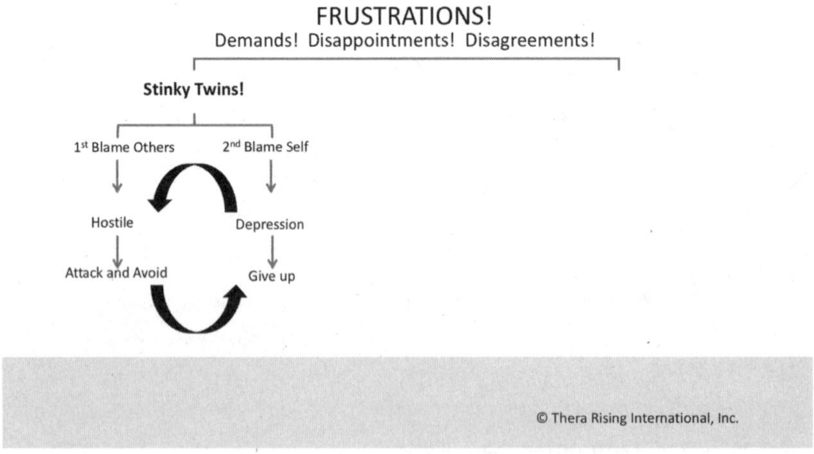

Figure 2.3. Blaming others can make blaming yourself more automatic.

Depression is considered a significant risk factor for heart disease in both men and women, and depression's toll on the body can also translate into a compromised immune system. Not only are depressed people more susceptible to colds and viruses, studies show that depression is also a risk factor for cancer. Although some forms of depression are the result of chemical imbalance, harsh self-criticism is a major contributor.

Cancer and heart disease are the two biggest killers in modern society, and we can substantially lower our risk for both by paying attention to how we think when we face frustration. Clearly, we need to access tools that bring relief.

The Stinky Twins

I call First Assumption (blaming others) and Second Assumption (blaming self) the Stinky Twins. They consist of the same "DNA" or thinking patterns. "I'm frustrated because of someone's stupidity!" The only difference is the target of contempt.

They are "stinky" because, in addition to being harmful to our health, they are 100 percent ineffective in solving problems. Hence, problems accumulate and weigh us down, and they lead to increased feelings of hopelessness. When we feel contempt for others, it may be to relieve the despair that accompanies self-loathing.

The flooded boss

Let's look at an example of how outer and inner blame are linked. Imagine I'm a vice president who knows nothing about flooding and its dire consequences. I flood frequently—after all, once in a while I deserve an outburst! I've earned it, and you're not going to deny me the right to express my indignation about sloppy work! I shouldn't have to put up with inefficiencies and apathy!

During a hectic day, when nerves are frayed, one of my direct reports, Megan, warily tells me that her presentation to the executive team will have to be rescheduled because of problems with the new software. I explode and tell her I've just about had it with her poor planning! Even if Megan's been warned that I flood, she will be hurt by my tirade. However, because my ability to problem solve and be attentive is impaired, I will not care about Megan's feelings or notice her reactions.

I will be pumped up, but my tirade carries a big, hidden price. My irrational response will destroy her willingness to exceed my expectations for the sheer pleasure of pleasing someone she respects and trusts. Her passion, her opinion of me, and her pride are in jeopardy.

However, I might bumble ahead and inflict even more damage as a consequence of my self-righteous behavior. I could turn my contempt and inflammatory thinking on myself. (In the next paragraph, notice how I inflame the situation with words that exaggerate the impact of my behavior.)

"I'm such a lousy supervisor. Why did I jump on her like that? This is *my* fault; she's only been here six months. I knew this assignment was a stretch for her, and I should have paid more attention to her progress. I hope she doesn't resign. I'd hate to lose *another* direct report this year. I'm lousy at supervising people. I never should have taken this promotion."

Blame has now turned on me. What's the quickest way to buffer my self loathing? I can turn the arrow of blame toward the IT department or the person responsible for designing the software. Pumped up with renewed motivation, I stop the IT director in the hall and make poorly informed accusations against his group, which angers the director and his staff. I might feel terrible, but now I have energy!

I could use my attack on the IT department as a way of smoothing over the situation with Megan. I could apologize and tell her the problem is really their fault. Although she might feel relieved that she is no longer my target, at a deep, unexpressed level, she no longer trusts me.

The most tragic outcome of swinging back and forth between inner and outer blame is that the resulting isolation, hostility, and self-criticism will keep me from focusing on the problem: the software program needs attention. However, I have alienated the IT department and Megan—the people I need to solve the problem.

In addition, my hostile attacks will damage her self-confidence. To soothe her nervous system, she'll tell others about my hostile reaction, and they will be empathic to her embarrassment by telling stories about their run-ins with me.

At some level, I know *I* am the topic of office gossip. Why is the organization turning against me?! Now I am even more vulnerable to depression and aggression.

Chronic anger and fragile self-esteem

What causes chronic anger? Although many factors come into play, Dr. Redford Williams concluded that cynicism, or a general mistrust of other people's motives, fuels hostility.

Cynicism is not skepticism. Skepticism is occasional doubt with specific individuals. Cynicism is widespread mistrust of other people's motives. It's an attitude similar to, "I don't trust anyone but you and me, Dick, and I'm starting to worry about you!" It's contempt *before* investigation.

What causes cynicism? Think of the most cynical person you know. Does fragile self-esteem fit? Could anger and cynicism help individuals fend off threats to their self-worth?

Ohio State University's Jennifer Crocker presented her findings at a Cortex CEU seminar and said that individuals who have unstable and inflated feelings of self-worth (not grounded in objective measures) are the most likely to become hostile, defensive, and aggressive when they are challenged or disappointed.

Individuals with unstable or fragile self-esteem base their feelings of worthiness on other people's opinions, and the success or failure of their efforts, moment to moment. Even though their esteem scores are average or above, when disappointed or confronted, they react aggressively. Chronic anger can be a reaction to a deep, underlying fear that others will judge us as worthless.

Naomi Eisenberger of the University of California, Los Angeles, has shown that "socially painful experiences such as exclusion or rejection are processed in the same neural regions that process pain." In other words, social pain literally hurts.

Hostility can be a smoke screen behind which people hide their feelings of self-contempt, and defend their identities.

Nastiness can be a mask for a person's insecurities. Kindness penetrates that.

—Judy Orloff, MD

Imagine you have a very cynical direct report named Beatrice who always complains about change. As you arrive at work, she is fuming about the sudden addition of several new products.

If you decide that she is unappreciative of what it takes to stay in business, you will mirror her negativity and feel annoyed. However, if you consider that her complaints might be due to lack of confidence or anxiety about not measuring up, your attitude might shift. Your reaction might be similar to "Come on, Beatrice, pull up the new product guide and I'll walk you through it."

When I deal with chronically defensive and blaming clients, I always start with the assumption that self-confidence is at the core of the issue. I assume that this person is attempting to defend their sense of self-worth. This thought keeps me from getting hooked by their contempt. I try to dig down and respond to their predicament with assertiveness but also warmth.

As we'll see later, if our goal is to bring about change, kindness combined with high expectations is very effective.

The grand dragon and the cantor

After I read Dr. Williams's and Dr. Crocker's work about the relationship between self-esteem and aggression, I began to look for examples of how fragile, unstable self-esteem responds to kindness rather than confrontation.

There is an extraordinary example in the true story of Larry Trapp, the former grand dragon of the White Knights of the Ku Klux Klan of Nebraska, and the Weisser family. Although there are many more recent stories (e.g., *Rising Out of Hatred* by Eli Saslow) the Trapp/Weisser account is especially illuminating. This story about a duel between positive and negative energy is one of the most enlightening chronicles of the last century. If we are serious about reducing the amount of hostility in our world and workplaces, the Weisser's experience sheds light on what works. The story is the basis of Kathryn Watterson's award-winning book *Not by the Sword: How a Cantor and His Family Transformed a Klansman.*

Larry Trapp is an example of someone at the far left end of the emotional continuum introduced in the previous chapter. As a grand dragon,

Larry spent his days in Lincoln, Nebraska, sending out hate mail, sponsoring racist videos on cable TV, and organizing fellow Klansmen and white supremacists to target and terrorize African Americans, Jews, Asians, Hispanics, Indians, gays, and lesbians.

One of the families Larry Trapp terrorized was the local cantor and acting rabbi, Michael Weisser, and his wife, Julie. Larry's harassment started when he called the Weisser's house with the following threat: "You'll be sorry you ever moved to Randolph Street, Jew boy." Later, he sent a note: "The KKK is watching."

Figure 2.4. Larry Trapp in Klan regalia. Used with permission from Kathryn Watterson.

Michael and Julie are examples of individuals at the right end of the continuum whose warmth and skill created an extraordinary ability to transform destructive behavior.

Larry's first threatening phone call to the Weisser household shocked and angered the couple. But Michael was used to confronting prejudice and hostility in his work as the leader of their small synagogue. Michael's anger gradually turned to curiosity about Larry, and later to concern.

Michael started to call Larry and leave messages meant to make Larry think. He wanted to connect with Larry and explore his rationale and the experiences that led him to his rage. Other messages were from Michael's heart, such as, "Larry, if you ever get tired of hating, there's a whole world of love waiting for you."

Both Michael and Julie tempered their conversations with practical offers to help Larry in any way they could. Slowly Larry's attitude began to shift; he wasn't used to warmth and kindness, and it disarmed him.

After months of intense phone conversations, Michael received a call that was unlike any other. Larry said bluntly, "I want to get out, but I don't know how." Larry was beginning to link hostility with his poor health. "I'm feeling confused and kind of sick. I think this is making me sick." Michael had been asking Larry if he would be willing to talk face to face, and now Larry finally agreed. Michael and Julie told Larry they'd meet him at his apartment and bring a bucket of chicken from KFC.

When Julie and Michael arrived at Larry's apartment, they were disheartened by the reality of what lay behind the smoke screen of hostiity. Larry was an unkempt, partially blind, disheveled man. He sat in a wheelchair, having lost both of his lower legs to diabetes. He was sitting alone in a barren, dirty room surrounded by guns, hate literature, bomb-making supplies, and Nazi paraphernalia.

Larry's rage kept introspection and depression at bay.
—Kathryn Watterson, *Not by the Sword*

Michael reached out to shake hands with Larry, and Larry began to sob. Underneath his rage, he was exhausted and feeling hopeless about his future. His misery and isolation were intensified because the energy Larry invested in targeting and harassing others was blocking positive relationships with people who might befriend him.

During their fateful conversation, Larry apologized repeatedly for terrorizing and hurting others. The next day, Larry resigned from the

Klan even though he knew that he might be killed. Shortly afterward he began the long process of meeting face to face with people he had terrorized and asking for their forgiveness.

The local paper ran an article on the story of the grand dragon and the cantor, which was picked up by the Associated Press, the *New York Times,* and *Time* magazine. There was a flurry of activity and interviews, but behind the scenes, Julie and Michael continued to quietly bring Larry home-cooked meals and medicine, and provide rides to his doctor.

Figure 2.5. Larry Trapp and the Weisser family. Reprinted with permission from Barry Staver.

Several months and many trips later, it became clear that Larry was dying. The Weisser family asked Larry if he wanted to become part of their family. When Larry said yes, one of the Weisser's adolescent daughters moved to the basement, and Larry took up residence in her former bedroom.

In response to this loving family, Larry abandoned his hate-filled habits. He moved in the opposite direction and made amends, acknowledged the harm he had inflicted on innocent families, and encouraged other Klan members to leave the organization.

Eventually, Larry asked Michael to teach him Hebrew, and before he died, he converted to Judaism.

Hostility brought Larry relief from self-loathing

One of the most disturbing, yet revealing aspects of the Weisser/Trapp story occurred just before Larry's death. During his Klan days, Larry professed his hatred for African Americans claiming he had been gang raped by a group of black adolescents at reform school.

However, in his last confession to Julie, the one that was most difficult for him to make, Larry admitted that he hadn't been raped. As a young man, he had consensual sex with an African-American male. Larry, who had been raised with intolerance and contempt, judged himself mercilessly and turned his inner hostility into outer hatred as a means to feel relief from self-loathing. Michael and Julie were witnessing someone trying to salvage a fragile sense of self worth. This is a classic example of the cycle we discussed in the early pages of this chapter about First and Second Assumptions.

Similar to most people caught in this trap, Larry became increasingly depressed as he learned that targeting and despising other people didn't bring him the respect and peace of mind he craved.

When Larry met the Weisser family, he was at a turning point. His deteriorating health made it undeniably clear that he didn't have much time to get it right. When Julie and Michael offered their friendship, Larry dropped his hostility in order to embrace an opportunity to be loved.

Hostility collapses into hopelessness and despair

On a much less dramatic scale, I have seen this exact dynamic as I work with teams incapacitated by internal hostility and conflict. When I come into an organization to resolve conflict, team members are surprisingly eager to cooperate. The initial rush of hostility they felt at the onset of their escalated conflict has faded into hopelessness. Team members are exhausted from tension, and they ache for positive interactions and the respect of their supervisors and peers. All of us are robbed of our primary desires—achievement and camaraderie—when hostility is a primary means of energy.

Contempt doesn't have boundaries

Employees mirror the habits of leadership. When leaders tolerate and model First Assumption, they lose control over how pervasive it becomes.

I witnessed this firsthand when a Twin Cities nonprofit asked for my help. Their organization worked for better environmental laws, and their primary activities included raising money and lobbying legislators. A significant percentage of their employees were volunteers, and the organization fell into the trap of demonizing groups to keep their staff motivated.

Instead of talking about the concerns and interests of farmers, they inflated the situation and referred to them as "greedy farmers." Politicians became "corrupt politicians." However, as always, this thinking pattern didn't stop when employees returned to the office after fundraising or meeting with legislators. Their reactive and inflammatory way of thinking crept into the workplace, and their organization became noticeably more uncivil.

In the planning stages of our project, Michelle, the company president, and I previewed the seminar concepts (First, Second, and Third Assumptions; inflammatory thinking; and flooding), and I could see she was experiencing a watershed moment. She told me these concepts were exactly what the group needed, so we scheduled two sessions with the entire staff.

These employees were bright and passionate. Similar to their president's response, they ate this material up. The next day we followed up with a Code of Conduct session in which they identified specific, problematic norms they pledged to change as a group.

I kept in touch with the president for several years and the new way of problem-solving, along with the interaction with each other and their key stakeholders, solidified the new cultural norm.

I have yet to find anyone in the workplace who chooses hostility if the energy of connectedness is available. It's only in the void of positive energy that anger and belittling others appeals.

Send the Stinky Twins to reform school

In the next chapter we'll find an abundance of good news as we focus on Third Assumption, the situation-based, analytical response to frustrations and disagreements. We will finish three previous stories and discover that when we lose interest in First and Second Assumptions, we make a dramatic shift toward better health, effectiveness, and self-confidence. We'll look at the analytical response to the economic depression after World War I, the reason Tony's boss moved the facility to his hometown, and why the driver neglected to pay attention to the green light.

During seminars, individuals are engrossed in the information about flooding, the amygdala, the cortex, heart disease, and inner and outer contempt. However, there is typically a palpable sense of relief when we turn our attention to Third Assumption, the thinking pattern that produces thriving workplace cultures.

Although First Assumption and negative climates are fascinating, they cannot sustain us. For optimal, long-term performance, we must make a commitment to create cultures in which energy can be continuously renewed. Our longing for positive communities is ancient and unfailing.

"I don't know what to say," Larry said between more tears. "I've been so terrible to you and to so many people. I can't believe I hated you so much. How can you ever forgive me?"

"We do forgive you," Julie said. "We do."

"I don't know what, but I . . . I just feel different." Larry said, putting the palm of his hand on his stomach. "I've never felt like this before."

—Kathryn Watterson, *Not by the Sword*

3

The Reflective Assumption: A Pathway to Dialogue and Data

"The arrival of a good clown exercises a more beneficial influence upon the health of a town than the arrival of twenty asses laded with drugs."

—John Sydenham, 17th-century physician

As you know, when we use First Assumption, we're concluding, "A mindless idiot is making my life miserable!" and we latch onto a trait (age, gender, political views, ethnicity, IQ) to identify *their* responsibility for *our* frustration. Second Assumption is even more personally damaging as we blame and inflame anger that is turned inward.

In Third Assumption, we presume that the other person is reasonable, and once we know the whole story, his or her behavior will make sense. Emotionally, we are curious about their hidden reality. This assumption shapes both the manner in which we approach the individual and the subsequent likelihood of a positive outcome. We are more effective, because resisting the urge to flood when situations run amuck endears us to others.

In Third Assumption brain activity occurs in the cortex, the problem-solving engine of the brain. This thinking is analytical and rational. It considers options and possibilities. This attitude brings us closer to the heart rhythms of appreciation from Chapter One, which are associated with increased creativity and mental clarity.

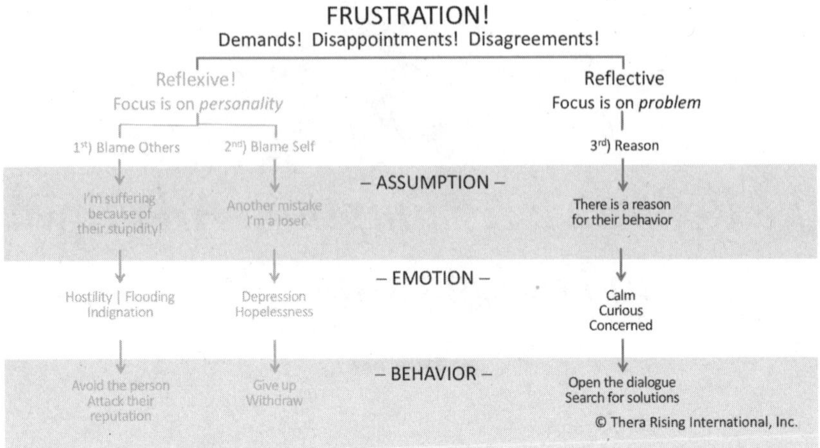

Figure 3.1. Third Assumption, the reflective reaction of looking for reasons.

Clearly, our guesses about the cause of our disagreement shape our behavior. When we react using First Assumption, we attack and avoid. Under the spell of Second Assumption we disengage, sulk, or become paralyzed. Only in Third Assumption do we seek out the other party and initiate a conversation. Third Assumption is the cognitive pathway to dialogue and data.

The Roosevelt administration: Third Assumption—almost

At times we can see the impact of these thinking patterns on micro scales, where only one or two individuals are involved. In other scenarios, the impact is macro and involves entire nations. As a means to contrast the effectiveness of different assumptions, let's return to the Great Depression.

In Chapter Two we used Hitler as an example of a First Assumption leader. While he was obsessed with categorizing *people* as the source of Germany's financial stagnation, the United States focused on initiatives to stimulate the economy, and the dearth of regulations in the banking industry and the stock market. When Roosevelt's administration acted with Third Assumption, Congress passed more legislation to shore up the economy in his first 100 days in office than any presidency in history.

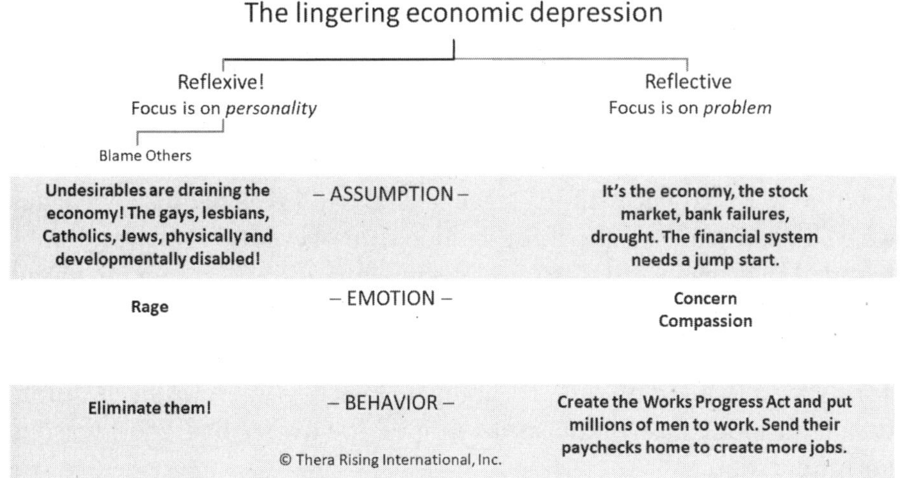

The lingering economic depression
Reflexive!
Focus is on *personality*
Reflective
Focus is on *problem*
Blame Others
Undesirables are draining the economy! The gays, lesbians, Catholics, Jews, physically and developmentally disabled!
– ASSUMPTION –
It's the economy, the stock market, bank failures, drought. The financial system needs a jump start.
Rage
– EMOTION –
Concern
Compassion
Eliminate them!
– BEHAVIOR –
Create the Works Progress Act and put millions of men to work. Send their paychecks home to create more jobs.
© Thera Rising International, Inc.

Figure 3.2. The lingering economic depression and Hitler's and Roosevelt's reaction.

Among many initiatives, the US government started the Public Works Administration and the Civilian Conservation Corps. By putting millions of men back to work, these programs jump-started the economy. With the exception of pocket money, the worker's pay was sent to families for food, transportation, and clothing, which further stimulated economic activity. These workers built thousands of bridges, buildings, and roads on public land, and examples of their work still exist today.

However, there is a notable exception to Third Assumption thinking in the United States. After the bombing of Pearl Harbor, more than 110,000 Japanese-Americans were sent to internment camps. We can clearly see the impact of the amygdala on our nation's assumptions and policies following the destruction of the US naval fleet.

Tony's termination

At the micro level, let's return to the story from Chapter Two about Tony and his boss's decision to move the plant to South Carolina. After the surprise announcement, most of Tony's colleagues went on a "search for stupidity" about who to blame for the relocation. They alienated people (engineering, marketing, the owner) and damaged the very relationships they needed to address the problem of searching for new employment.

Contrast their reactions with Tony's calm, reflective response. After making the rounds to various departments, Tony went back to his office, closed the door, updated his resume, and wrote several cover letters. Later he went to chat with his legal assistant and realized his colleagues were still complaining about the sudden turn of events. Tony was dumbfounded that they were wasting precious time instead of moving ahead and taking care of business.

By tapping into Third Assumption thinking instead of "awfulizing," Tony stayed focused on *task*. He accepted the corporate closing as unfortunate but not catastrophic, and assumed the owner had good reasons for his decision.

In fact, within a year of the president's departure, Tony learned that his former boss had died from cancer. The president had most likely returned home in anticipation of a long struggle with his health.

Tony's assumption allowed him to move forward quickly with confidence and calm. Also, by not joining the criticism of the president, he was spared the subsequent embarrassment of many former employees when they learned that their former president had passed away.

Choose assumptions in ambiguous situations

Let's also return to the story about the oblivious driver as a means to contrast the impact of the three assumptions. In First Assumption, we assume the driver didn't move after the green light because she was too irresponsible or selfish to care about anyone but herself.

In Second Assumption, we inflame and blame ourselves: "I'm so short-tempered and disorganized. I *never* leave on time!"

In Third Assumption, we'll assume there's a *reason* the driver is focused on the back seat. In ambiguous situations we make a guess about what's going on. Why not tap assumptions that preserve our health and mood, and give us the best possibility of solving the problem? Thinking reflectively, from the cortex, allows reasons for her behavior to surface.

To avoid flooding, sometimes I'll distract my brain from blaming and inflaming by giving it an assignment: "Give me five reasons why a reasonable person would focus on the back seat instead of driving." The possibilities are limitless: the groceries spilled; she's lost, and her phone is on the floor in the back seat; she has asthma or diabetes, and she needs her medication; she's tending to a friend who is ill; or the cigarette she flipped out the window blew back in and the back seat is on fire!

During a seminar, when people switch from First to Third Assumption, they stop ridiculing the driver and joking at her expense. They become more reflective and concerned, and you can watch the influence of the cortex on their behavior. Individuals become empathic and tell stories about similar experiences in their lives. The behavior created in this contemplative mood is dramatically different than the self-righteous, aggressive energy of blame. This thinking pattern engenders compassion and a desire to be of assistance.

"BIBS"

The story of the "oblivious driver" is true. After the incident, the driver wrote a letter to the editor of the local paper. In it she described how the man behind her flooded, shook his fist, swore, and blasted his horn.

The reason she hadn't moved when the light changed was because her toddler, who was in the back seat, was choking, and she was frantically trying to clear her trachea. *Of course* she ignored the green light. This example highlights another reason to avoid First Assumption. When we flood, not only are we useless, we can also make the problem worse.

To override the negativity bias of the brain and focus on hidden reasons, we use the term "baby in the back seat" as a shorthand way of reminding ourselves to become curious about constraints or pressures that might be hidden from view.

In the workplace, there are thousands of "babies in the back seat," such as materials shortages, rapidly shifting customer preferences, lack of information, process problems, shareholder pressure, resource cuts, union constraints, lack of skill, lack of insight, OSHA restrictions, etc.

There's an easy way to remember the three assumptions. Reflexive reactions are the Stinky Twins, Blame Others and Blame Self, and Third Assumption (the reflective response) becomes "BIBS" or "Baby in the back seat." These terms become mnemonics, or prompts within teams and across organizations. More than one CEO has told me that when he or she is confronted with a crises, they use the phrase "Baby in the back seat" to consciously shape their thinking, avoid shooting the messenger, and flooding.

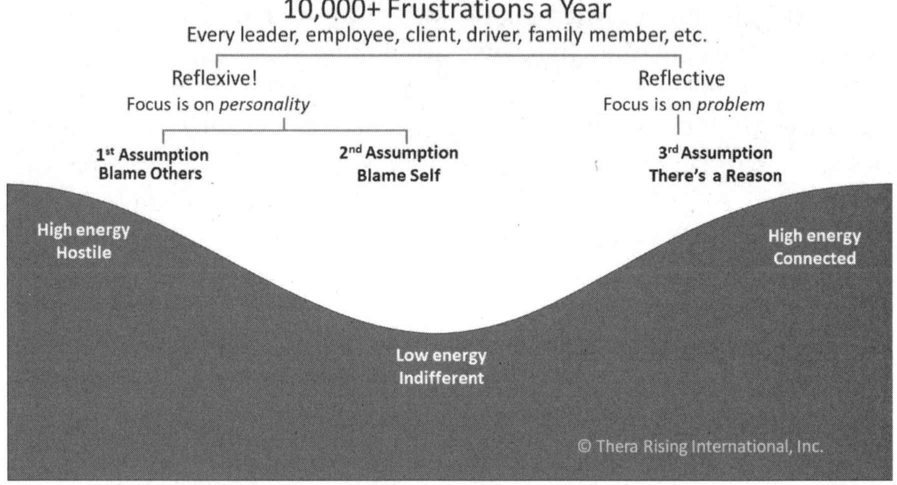

Figure 3.3. Thinking patterns create cultures.

An average of thirty frustrations, or mini-crises, a day accumulates to more than 10,000 in a year's time. And *everyone* is struggling—every leader, employee, client, driver, and so on. *The individual and collective response to frustration determines culture,* not the amount of external pressure, profitability, or the shenanigans of the competition.

We can combine the two mental models, "Three Cultures at Work" and "Frustration." If groups adopt First Assumption thinking, their cultures are dominated by fear, mistrust, and hostility. When Second Assumption is the primary response to frustration, teams lose energy and disengage. Third Assumption is the only response that creates the possibility of resiliency and cohesiveness during disagreement and stress.

Pause to think about what it's like when we face aggravations *without* blame, pulling together during moments of crises, bonding for having weathered the storm, and optimizing opportunities.

The repercussions of these ongoing assumptions can't be overstated.

Connectedness—nature's antidote to stress

Although it is true that nature uses the negativity bias of the brain to keep us alert and safe, our bodies also have a built-in reward system for bonding and affiliating with others. Our cells crave connectedness from birth and this positive energy is a life-long form of cellular nourishment.

In her bestselling book *Love 2.0,* Barbara Fredrickson, PhD, the Director of Positive Emotions and Psychophysiology Laboratory at the University of North Carolina, details findings on the physiology of love. Fredrickson and others use biochemicals and images of brain activity from fMRIs (Functional Magnetic Resonance Imaging) to understand the conditions and experience of connectedness.

Most of us were socialized to believe that we only love a few individuals in our lives. We expect that close relationships are achievable after many months or years of investment and intimacy.

However, using data on how our bodies react to emotions, Fredrickson has developed an entirely new understanding of what constitutes the sensations of love.

Feelings of connection are associated with the biochemicals of dopamine (which triggers increases in energy, drive, and concentration) oxytocin (the bonding chemical released during sexual activity and breastfeeding), and serotonin (a mood stabilizer that can thwart depression). Our bodies deeply crave these emotional states; Fredrickson calls them an indispensable source of energy. When two individuals are connecting, it doesn't take much time before these chemicals are released and brainwaves synchronize. Even a warm, intimate conversation with a stranger on a plane will suffice if the interaction meets certain criteria.

The conditions that cause the sense of closeness aren't complicated, but they are becoming more elusive as our world becomes more electronic and less face to face. Because so much information is communicated beyond the actual words a speaker is using, in order to interpret a speaker's intentions, we rely on voice tone and facial expressions. Psychologist Paul Eckman and his colleagues have discovered hundreds of muscles in our faces that don't move unless we genuinely feel the emotion. If we try to mask our true feelings, the other party can discern insincerity through our facial expressions.

For instance, if I were feigning that I was thrilled *you* won a multimillion-dollar lottery prize instead of me, you would sense that my congratulations were insincere. You might not know why you felt uneasy and skeptical, but my inability to fake my delight would be conveyed by what Ekman calls "micro-emotions" that flash across my face. You might unconsciously discern insincerity through subtle signals that will defeat my attempt to deceive you.

Connectedness comes from sharing one or more positive emotions, mirroring of behaviors and biochemistry, and a mutual interest in each other's well-being. When these conditions are present we experience a sense of intimacy. This is critical, because in a world of frustration, frequent and genuine bonding allows teams to bear disagreement without breaking into adversarial factions.

Fredrickson concluded that the need for closeness is lifelong. Without a steady stream of connection, we struggle with a sense of isolation, even feelings of rejection. Without closeness, we begin to look for substitutes such as too much TV, gossip, alcohol, drugs, comfort food, or an unhealthy overinvestment in work. A meta-analysis found that living with loneliness increases the risk of dying early by 45 percent (Holt-Lunstad, 2015).

After we presented this material in a seminar, my son Ben, who is a Thera Rising associate, was chatting with an attendee named Tim. Tim confided that in his previous job, which he described as fairly bleak, he attended one "soul-sucking" meeting after another. He told Ben that during his tenure at this company, "I never drank so much alcohol or watched so much TV." After leaving the company and securing a more engaging position with colleagues who also valued connectedness, he said he effortlessly ceased both excessive behaviors.

Feeling awkward is a signal to meet face to face

When we find ourselves in an awkward situation that requires skill and tact, we should make every effort to meet face to face. A program like Skype would be a reasonable alternative as it provides both visual and auditory information that allows recipients to discern our intentions. If that's not practical, a phone call will lead to less misunderstandings than text or email, which should be reserved only for communicating discrete facts, such as "The meeting is Wednesday at 3:30."

There is no need for us to take these kinds of risks with our relationships. Remember: *everyone* is struggling to compensate for the negativity bias of the brain and to accurately interpret the behavior they witness. Recognize how important it is to engage face to face, and do yourself, and the people in your life, a favor that will pay off on many levels. In Chapter Ten, we'll cover an effective way to open the dialogue on just about any issue.

Firefighters—courageous and connected

One of the professions that takes connection seriously is firefighting. Any profession that puts people in harm's way in order to do a job must have high levels of camaraderie. When firefighters are dragging hoses into an uncontrolled blaze, they need to know that their partners are invested in their well-being.

The first time I presented the material on connectedness, the audience was a group of firefighters. I was nervous and wondered how a group of burly men would respond. I shouldn't have worried; they were way ahead of me.

I learned that fire stations organize food drives for the community and participate in Toys for Tots. They celebrate every holiday, continuously cook for each other, run safety camps, and spray down delighted kids with their hoses during "National Night Out" gatherings.

One of their connecting habits that most impressed me is their debriefing after every incident. Regardless of the nature of the call, back at the station crews talk about what went right and what they could have done differently. They acknowledge how individual reactions contributed to the success of the team. This atmosphere of recognition and appreciation is one the best ways to de-stress and reinforce connection.

The helper's high

Kindness is another reliable way to positively enrich our lives. In some situations we can benefit from the chemicals of both connectedness and the helper's high, which is similar to the runner's high, except without sweating!

Allan Luks, the director of Big Brothers Big Sisters of New York, teamed up with biopsychologist Howard Andrews to investigate the effect of volunteer work on health. They found that people who volunteered on a regular basis experienced an increase in endorphins, one of the body's pleasure chemicals. Luks dubbed this the "helper's high." Unfortunately, at the end of a long run, endorphins drop rapidly, resulting in a slide from a runner's high to fatigue. However, with the helper's high, there are "long-lasting feelings of euphoria, followed by relief from symptoms like lupus and arthritis." The feeling of euphoria occurs through the release of endorphins (the body's naturally produced morphine) which are no cost, no-risk opiates.

Our bodies are wired to feel good when we treat each other with kindness and compassion. This is nature's way of rewarding us. "Yes! Do more of this. Helping others is good for your survival and the survival of your species."

Although Luks found that we experience the biggest endorphin release when we do volunteer work, he also found health is positively affected by simple acts of kindness, such as pitching in to help a colleague meet a deadline.

Helping can trigger post-traumatic growth

Altruism matters even in the face of catastrophe, not only for the recipients, but also for the volunteers. There have been several studies on post-traumatic growth and the possibility, not only of recovering from trauma, but reporting higher life satisfaction because of it. I was particularly impressed by a study done in New York City after the terrorist attacks on September 11th, 2001.

Three years after the towers fell, mental health professionals noted different levels of emotional recovery and resiliency in New York City residents. Not surprisingly, many New Yorkers were still struggling.

However, a subset of survivors reported *more* life satisfaction. When researchers looked at what made the difference, NYC residents who reported emotional growth had refused to retreat as a result of the devastation. They reached out, took advantage of social and psychological resources available, and volunteered. Trauma pushed them out the door to help others. Individuals who reported post-traumatic growth grew in appreciation, intimacy with partners and family, creativity, and spirituality (Tedeschi and Calhoun, 2004).

The more our bodies relax into feelings of connectedness, the less we'll feel vulnerable to feelings of isolation and rejection. The more stable and connected we feel, the more resilient we become. We are less likely to flood or treat others with contempt. Cohesiveness and connectedness are essential sources of energy and antidotes to disengagement, anger, and stress.

Think about changes you can make to add more connectedness and kindness to your life. If true connectedness requires mutual concern for each other's well-being, eye contact, and hearing the other person's voice, how many minutes per week do you actually have access to moments of belonging?

When have *you* felt connected at work? What are the conditions of these experiences? How can you increase connectedness in your work as an individual or group?

The best experiences of connectedness and the helper's high are woven into the fabric of the organization, not tacked on as an afterthought. I saw this happen in a hospital auditorium full of head nurses. The administration regularly brought in a former patient to speak to this group. About six months prior to this meeting, the speaker had arrived by ambulance while experiencing a heart attack. For roughly twenty minutes he talked about how anxious he had been, and the many acts of kindness he experienced from the hospital staff. Nurses are a tough audience, but for the entire time he spoke, there wasn't a sound in the room other than his voice.

We can make a habit of connecting with our colleagues, leadership, customers, vendors, and partners. Remember, the conditions of connection are mutual investment in each other's well-being, and the ability to see and hear each other.

As Barbara Fredrickson writes, "When you especially resonate with someone else . . . the two of you are quite literally on the same wavelength, biologically."

The benefits of appreciation and affection

I want to return to the discussion about emotions and health. If hostility and depression have negative impacts on health, does appreciation have a positive effect? At the positive end of the continuum, all the news is good.

Love is intimately related to health.
—Larry Dossey, MD

You probably know individuals who are energized by love. Their faces become more beautiful as they age. It lends another interpretation to Coco Chanel's phrase, "By the time you're fifty, you have the face you deserve." Her observation is true not only for people whose lives are dominated by negative energy, but also for people who thrive on love and connectedness.

For instance, researchers who scanned emergency room data discovered that heart attack victims who arrived at the hospital with family or friends were three times more likely to survive than people who came in alone.

In one of the first studies of the relationship between social support and health, Stanford psychiatrist David Spiegel studied women with terminal breast cancer. He divided the patients in half. One group met twice a week to talk about their fears and obtain support from other patients. In the final stages of the disease, they were a tightly knit community, and their friendships extended beyond their scheduled meetings.

Spiegel waited two years to analyze the final data and said, "I almost fell off my chair when I read the study's outcomes." The group that developed intense emotional connection lived twice as long as the group without support. A small, nonchemical intervention had significantly prolonged the lives of the women in support groups.

Caring is biological.
—James Lynch, University of Maryland

Emotions and the immune system

Researchers at HeartMath asked students to focus for five minutes on sincere care, or a peak experience. Their immune systems functioned at a higher level for six hours! If this dramatic impact on the immune system is found with people who simply *remember* a positive experience, imagine the impact when we experience these events in real time.

Since learning about this research, I've adopted a ritual. In the morning, before I get out of bed, and at night before I fall asleep, I consciously think of someone I love, or things for which I am grateful. These two, five-minute periods in combination boost my immune system for a total of twelve hours! During a Minnesota winter, generating feelings of appreciation is as easy as thinking about the thermostat that turns up the heat before I get out of bed. I also gained an unexpected return. I rewired my brain and now I can feel the energy of appreciation throughout the day.

Our most elevated moods occur in relationships of affection and emotional safety, and we are intrinsically motivated to seek out feelings of well-being through acts of kindness. Consequently, I have found the most miserable people in the workplace are those who are cut off from the feelings of camaraderie through conflict or isolation.

We can generate positive feelings on a crowded airplane, during a tense meeting with a vendor, or backed up in traffic. If we wire our brains to see the world through a lens of abundance, the benefits will affect strangers, our families, colleagues, and customers. Like Bruce, the veteran from Chapter Two, we are able to create feelings of serenity at will.

Wealth and well-being: John D. Rockefeller

This story about John D. Rockefeller Sr. is a little-known example of the link between emotions and health.

Rockefeller worked relentlessly until his early thirties, when he earned his first million. Ten years later he was at the head of the world's largest business, and became a billionaire at age fifty-three.

However, Rockefeller's business practices were so ruthless that he made countless enemies. Oil field workers hanged him in effigy, and he needed full-time bodyguards. Rockefeller could barely eat or sleep. He developed alopecia, a condition that results in the loss of body hair. He was so weak that his medical team predicted he'd only live another year. Doctors told him to get his affairs in order.

Although he had taken philanthropy seriously throughout his life, with his dire medical prognosis, he began giving money away in earnest. Through the Rockefeller Foundation, he underwrote hospitals, universities, and medical research that led to cures for tuberculosis, malaria, yellow fever, diphtheria, and hookworm.

As Rockefeller became more altruistic and connected to—rather than rejected by—society, his health issues started to resolve. His ability to eat, digest, and sleep improved, and he regained his vitality. Rather than dying at middle age as his doctors had feared, he lived to be ninety-seven years old!

There are many reasons to become skilled at creating feelings of appreciation, engage in altruistic behavior, and use Third Assumption in reaction to frustration. Our responses not only affect our success at work, but also the quality of our personal lives, including whether or not individuals are available to support us during personal or professional crisis. In combination, these factors are a significant asset, or a serious impediment, to our happiness and careers.

4

The Triggers and Costs of Adversarial Factions

"People who are talking to you about others,
are talking to others about you."
—Irish proverb

While teaching the following segment, more than one individual has burst out, "Why didn't someone tell me this before?!" Listening to the following material, many individuals find that the shoe *does* fit, and at some point in their careers, they have fallen into the trap of belonging to an adversarial faction.

In relationship to conflict escalation, "factions" have a negative connotation. Sometimes they're called power struggles or "politics." They are not your friendly neighborhood group banding together to spruce up the park. Adversarial factions, the ones we're addressing in this chapter, exist to raise one's status at the expense of another person or group.

It is not malice that drives us to engage in some of the following behaviors. None of us were warned that seemingly innocent accusations will become toxic and spread, how easily bystanders will be drawn into the fray, how the other party will mirror our behaviors, how the visibility and stakes of the tension will increase, how we will lose control over the trajectory, and how we will find ourselves judged harshly by the organization as our personal vendettas hobble productivity.

In this book we're focusing on workplace conflict, but you can discern similar patterns in every group: families, schools, government, neighborhoods, faith communities, nations, and so on.

This chapter is a cautionary tale based on a synthesis of many conflicts I've worked to resolve. Individuals can spend days or years in any one of these stages.

When we are involved in a conflict it seems excruciatingly unique and personal, but in reality, it escalates in nine very predictable stages.

Stage One: Disagreement and disappointment

Let's name our two protagonists, Jada, the head of marketing and sales, and Martin, the head of operations. For many years, their work was interdependent; they updated each other constantly on their department initiatives and ideas for new markets and products. They enjoyed each other's company and relied on each other for support and feedback.

Since human nature is deeply flawed, an unfortunate event is inevitable. At a staff meeting, Martin interrupts and talks over Jada, and she finds his words disrespectful and insensitive.

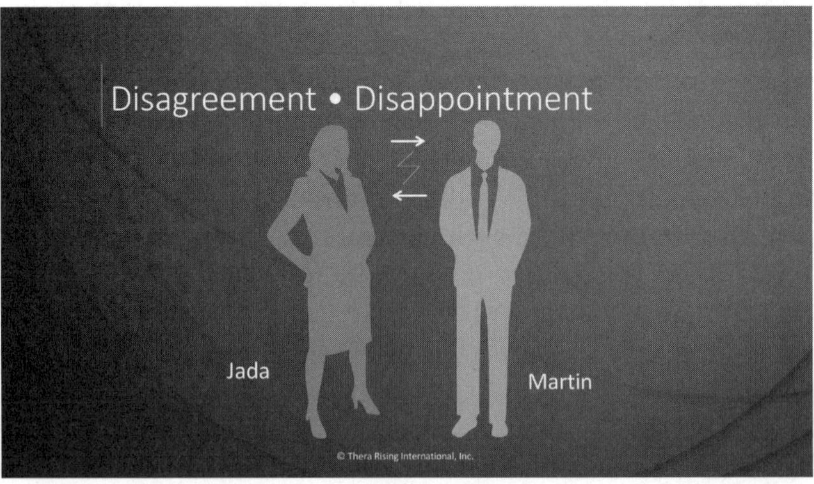

Figure 4.1. Disagreement and disappointment. If Jada and Martin don't open the dialogue, their relationship is at risk.

If Jada is highly skilled, she might say something on the spot, or soon after the meeting, and give Martin an opportunity to apologize and make amends. However, because she's taken aback by Martin's behavior, she fails to make her feelings known.

In reality, Jada is hurt. But a few hours later, her primary emotion will convert to anger, and her initial reaction will morph into self-righteous indignation.

Stage Two: Avoidance

When tension builds between two individuals, avoiding the other person seem like a low-risk option. We revert to this strategy because dodging others can be seen as an effective ploy in our personal lives.

We have probably all ducked neighbors, relatives, or friends with whom we no longer wish to connect. In our personal lives avoidance can seem like a no-risk strategy without messy repercussions. We hope to avoid an awkward conversation, a confrontation, or an exchange that makes the situation worse.

However, in the workplace, avoidance is a catastrophe. Work is interdependent, and the attempt to isolate ourselves from colleagues, direct reports, leaders, vendors etc., carries unforeseen consequences.

When we stop communicating, we are forced to move ahead in relative isolation. Decisions are made under the pressure of tight deadlines without the benefit of the other person's expertise. The estrangement becomes known throughout the organization, and the tension becomes a source of widespread gossip. Avoidance draws scrutiny, and rather than evading the spotlight, we find ourselves in the attention bullseye. Let me say it again: despite the superficial effectiveness of avoidance in our personal lives, in the workplace, dodging a colleague is *not* a low-risk behavior.

Stage Three: "I need to vent"

Martin and Jada's work requires that they coordinate their efforts and knowledge, yet they are no longer sharing information or engaging in meaningful conversations. Instead of helping each other problem solve, they start to cover up work-related difficulties. Finding themselves in a bind with lots of questions and no access to answers, they turn to an old standby—assumptions. And because of the negativity bias of the brain, their speculation will most likely take on a mistrustful tone.

Jada starts ruminating over bothersome concerns, such as, "Why isn't Martin doing something about our product shortage? Why hasn't he filled those two vacant positions? Why did he exclude me from a meeting I used to attend?" Under normal circumstances, she would learn the reasons for all these worries. But she has cut off her conduit to answers.

Martin is busy speculating in a similar vein about Jada. His nagging concerns sound like, "Where was Jada all of yesterday afternoon? Does she understand our products well enough to represent us at the conference? Is she talking about me when she's golfing with customers?"

I need to vent!
© Thera Rising International, Inc.

Figure 4.2. "I need to vent." Since Jada and Martin are no longer communicating, their frustration mounts.

When we deal with the anxiety generated by doubting another person's motives, and simultaneously avoiding them, venting is a natural reaction. We have to talk to *someone*. Consequently, Martin and Jada both begin talking *about* each other rather than talking *to* each other.

There are many forms of venting, but for our purpose, let's focus on drama-venting and define it using three dynamics. Drama-venting is a form of First Assumption because it is personality based and exaggerated, plus it is subtly intended to convince others to agree with our opinion and eventually join our faction. Over time, both Jada and Martin are incentivized to use First Assumption to build support for their conclusion that the other person or department is the problem.

When individuals vent, they present a biased and incomplete version of events. In a drama-venting the listener typically supports the person who is upset, and consequently, the speaker receives validation for their views.

Validating the perspective of someone who is venting seems harmless, but it is actually quite problematic. When leaders vent to their direct reports, employees are reluctant to contradict their bosses, and leaders believe they are boosting staff support. Unfortunately, this shady validation further inflames their indignation, and each person makes it their mission to bring down the other leader.

Not long ago, the field of psychology was deeply invested in encouraging people to vent. There was a decade or two when clients were given plastic bats and a pillow and encouraged to beat out their frustration. But scholarly research has shown that venting really doesn't help—and it actually makes us more aggressive.

However, like many individuals, Jada and Martin have not gotten the message. Consequently, Martin seeks out a colleague to share his negative speculations about Jada.

Martin will analyze Jada using a familiar dynamic: focusing on Jada's *personality* and labeling her. Often when we label others, we're invested in justifying our own behaviors and fortifying our faction.

When we're upset, it *does* helps to problem solve with a trusted colleague. However, that's a Third Assumption conversation that sounds remarkably different. The alternative to drama-venting is to seek the counsel of a wise colleague to help us address the problem. Presenting a balanced and accurate review of the facts is critical. If we're looking too good (innocent and righteous) when telling the story, we're probably still in First Assumption.

The following is an example of the difference between these two approaches. First, let's look at a situation in a drama-venting framework, and then see how much the picture changes when Martin does not focus on Jada's personality, paint her with a broad brush of contempt, recruit a faction member, or ignore his part in their flare-up.

In a drama-venting approach, Martin seeks out his colleague Raul. "Raul, do you have a minute? You won't *believe* what Jada did!"

Raul: "Nothing Jada does surprises me."

Martin: "This morning I presented an overview of our production schedule to the board based on Jada's sales figures. But halfway through my presentation, she interrupted and said, 'Martin, I think you are using sales estimates from the wrong quarter.'"

Raul: "Seriously?! What did you do?"

Martin: "It was incredibly awkward. I mumbled something about checking the data and getting back to the group by email. It was *so* embarrassing, and I'm pretty sure Jada kind of enjoyed it. Do you have problems with her too?"

Raul: "Seriously, dude, we *all* have problems with her. In fact, I heard that everyone in her department has checked out. They are so caught up in creating our digital presence they barely show up for the nitty-gritty of our operations meetings."

Martin: "I totally get it. Glad it's not just me. Well, I've got to run. Do you want to grab some pizza after work?"

Raul: "Sure. Maybe we can figure out how to take Jada down a peg."

Martin: "Awesome. Thanks, buddy!"

Let's walk through the same scenario using Third Assumption and a more analytical, problem-solving approach. Martin seeks out a trusted colleague and steps into his office.

Martin: "Raul, do you have a minute? I'm blown away by something that happened this morning at the board meeting."

Raul: "Really? I know that meeting was an opportunity for you to become more visible."

Martin: "I presented an overview of our production schedule based on Jada's sales figures. But halfway through she interrupted me and said, 'Martin, I think you're using the estimates from the first quarter, not second.'"

Raul: "Seriously?! Epic catastrophe!"

Martin: "Well I mumbled something about getting back to everyone after I checked the figures. And here's the worst part. When I pulled up the data, she was right!"

Raul: "No! How are you going to recover from *that* blunder?"

Martin: "Well, I'll talk to Jada first, and maybe we can figure out a reasonable next step. I am going to ask her if she'd coauthor an email to the board, with the correct data and a new schedule. I think it would create a sense of unity between Jada and me, rather than me sending it out and copying her."

Raul: "Great idea. I think that's a really classy way to go. Jada might also agree to coach you a bit on how they create projections. She is really good at what she does."

Martin: "If you have time, would you give me feedback on the first draft of the email?"

Raul: "No problem. Bring your laptop, and we'll grab some pizza after work."

The latter response will strengthen Martin's relationship with Jada; he will look polished in the eyes of the board, and he will gain the advantage of using her skills to improve his expertise.

Martin's first attempt had the potential to destroy his relationship with his colleague and forfeit an opportunity to grow his competencies.

There's also a hidden cost to Martin's First Assumption approach. When he was drama-venting, Raul went along with the Jada bashing, but Raul learned that Martin is a backstabber.

Raul will stop sharing his problems with Martin, and he might warn others that Martin throws his colleagues under the bus when they disagree.

Stage Four: Adversarial factions form

Factions are fascinating. The only person who doesn't typically belong to a faction is the CEO or president of the company. Individuals at the top of the hierarchy have access to enough data and information. The rest of us join alliances across the organization that supply us with chatter, speculation, and information leaks. Gossip is the currency of factions.

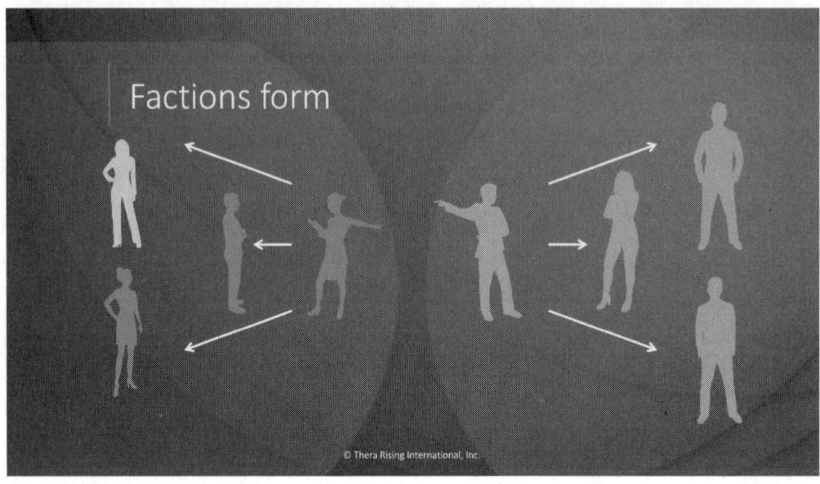

Figure 4.3. Factions form. Jada and Martin are building a group of loyalists at the expense of the other person.

Most of us belong to more than one faction, and we slip in and out depending on who we're with and the nature of our goals. The boundaries of factions are permeable, and sometimes allegiance to a specific faction is painfully short lived and can shift from conversation to conversation.

In the workplace, criticism of another person or department may be subtle, such as eye-rolling or an off-handed comment such as, "What can you expect?" Or it might be quite detailed and openly derogatory. This kind of negative speculation is some of the hottest gossip in organizations. It's been the source of many invitations to "close the door," so individuals can complain about others with impunity, or without fear of being overheard.

Stage Five: Negative speculation spreads and reaches the target

The worst is yet to come. After Raul and Martin's conversation, Raul has juicy gossip about their coworker, Jada. He runs into Becky, and with a slight twinge of conscience, Raul shares the conversation he just had with Martin. Perhaps he even embellishes what Martin said.

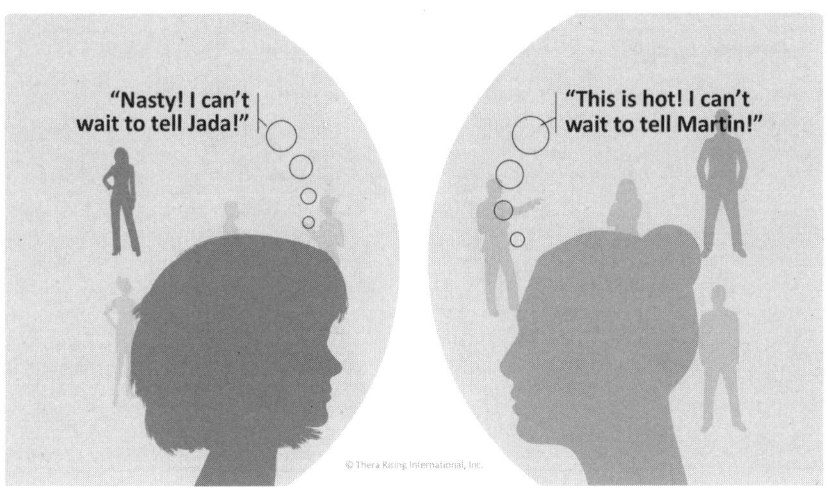

Figure 4.4. "Nasty!" Negative speculation and labeling leak between factions.

Becky will pass the negative speculation to another person, who will pass it along yet again. Eventually, the gossip gets back to the "target." When Jada learns what Martin is saying behind her back, she feels betrayed. She has lost trust in Martin and from here forward she will doubt anything he says. She emails Martin and cancels the meeting they had set up for that afternoon. Imagine the cost of this standoff!

Jada will attempt to change the organization's narrative about which person is more at fault for their estrangement. She will try to defend her reputation and status, and build her own faction for validation and support. Martin is matching her behavior step-by-step.

Jada and Martin are playing with fire. Social scientists have identified a curious phenomenon called the social evaluation threat (SET). SET is the fear that an important aspect of ourselves will be judged negatively by others. We worry that we will be powerless to protect our reputation and status from harm.

Similar to the negativity bias of the brain, this deeply seated apprehension can be traced to the hunting and gathering days. If you were ostracized during the time of this formative epoch, it meant certain death. We could not survive without the protection of our clan. Hence, we have

Figure 4.5. Both Jada and Martin feel betrayed when mean-spirited comments are conveyed back to them.

significant anxiety about being judged negatively by the people around us, and they have anxiety about being judged by *us*. This apprehension is both the backdrop to, and kindling for, the explosive nature of workplace gossip.

Martin, Jada, Raul, and Becky use negative speculations about others to attract loyalists, and to advance and protect their careers. Unknowingly, they are triggering an escalation of a small disagreement into a widening crisis over which they will now lose control.

Stage Six: Mistrust spreads to their groups

Whenever I listen to the stories of escalation, I'm struck by how distorted their speculations have become in contrast to the core decency of the individuals involved. They are loving parents, conscientious workers, and often morally mature human beings. Yet they are blind to the reality that although they feel like innocent victims, they are behaving like bullies. They inflame and misrepresent their case against the other party to justify their own behaviors.

At the end of a seminar, a professor approached me and said quietly, "You know what my takeaway is? I realized that although I've been exquisitely sensitive to people who have hurt me, I've been totally oblivious to the people I've hurt." What an eloquent insight into the bully/victim dynamic! Jada and Martin's behavior is driven by fear. They cannot discern that they are locked in a battle of their own making, in which they are equally complicit.

Because Jada and Martin are both leaders, it is highly likely they're venting to their direct reports. Despite facilitating hundreds of conflicts, only once have I worked with two managers who, prior to my arrival, made a mutual commitment to *not* draw others into their quarrel. Leaders are often under the illusion that they are bonding their team when they denigrate others. There are always plenty of differences to pull teams apart: team members disagree politically, they may be at loggerheads about the direction of the company, or they might squabble over work distribution. Bonding by denigrating a targeted group or individual seems to provide a moment of welcomed unity.

Direct reports are vulnerable to becoming faction members because they are eager to please and align with the boss. Once they sense tension between Jada and Martin, they want to do their part to protect their department. Employees start to bring leaders incomplete or prejudicial information designed to inflame the group's outrage. After all, this steady stream of gossip is the essential glue for factions. In the past, Martin and Jada might have dismissed negative speculation about the other party, but now cynical interpretations are welcomed and rewarded.

Martin might use his negative speculation not only to bond with his team but also to explain away his group's poor quarterly performance, or his blunder in front of the board. Some employees realize that tension with the other department might be used to *their* advantage. Just as Martin can explain away his misstep in front of the board by blaming Jada, employees will use the same strategy to justify their poor performance.

If Martin and Jada allow this rationalization to continue, they will soon face the declining performance of both teams. Now the stakes are much, much higher.

Stage Seven: Elevate

Jada is at her wits' end. Not only is she collecting evidence of misconduct in operations, her faction members are also validating her concerns. Performance is deteriorating in both departments—not only because Martin and Jada no longer share information, but also because their teams are constantly distracted by the escalating tension.

Finally, Jada has had enough, and she insists on seeing Shawn, the VP, in a preemptive strike. Jada's accusations about Martin's shenanigans are very compelling because she *truly believes* her version of the facts, and Jada has validation from a variety of sources! Her anxiety-laden bottom line to Shawn is: "You *must* do something! We all agree!"

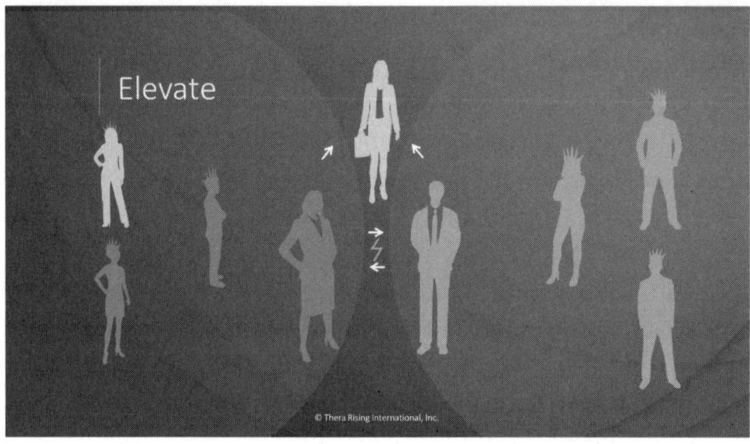

Figure 4.6. Elevate. "Boss, you have to do something!"

The VP is in a tough spot. When leaders are caught in the middle, they vacillate between shock that the situation has deteriorated so badly and concern that the employee's version of events is accurate. Cornered, and without a plan, most leaders will try to placate the complainer, weakly encourage Jada to talk to Martin, and rely on platitudes such as, "You're both valuable. Can't you just get along?"

Given that the organization is hypervigilant about this conflict, it won't be long before Martin learns that Jada was in a closed-door meeting for two hours with Shawn. What a threat!

He will contact Shawn and request a meeting at once! Martin is panicking and realizes he must meet with Shawn before she has a chance to spread Jada's concerns among the organization's leaders.

Martin presents a vastly different version of the story to Shawn, but he has the same basic demand. Again, the legitimacy of his interpretations are boosted by the fact that Martin *believes* his version of reality. "Everyone agrees that marketing is full of outliers. Shawn, you must do something. We've tried everything! We all agree!"

In my experience, leaders are totally unprepared for these situations (and subsequently, this is the topic of a popular Thera Rising seminar Conflict-Savvy Leader®). Being caught in the middle, between two direct reports, is not fun. Resolving a Stage Seven conflict requires specialized training and a fail-proof process.

However, in the moment, Shawn is adrift. She may stall, try to understand without agreeing, or explain to Martin why Jada feels the way she does. All of these reactions will fail.

If the conflict stalls at Stage Seven, Martin and Jada will carry ill will against each other for the rest of their careers. Without a skilled facilitator, the tension between them, and their departments, will fester.

Stage Eight: Termination

This unresolved, and now widespread, tension sets up the eighth stage. Shawn may reluctantly conclude that she has to terminate one of the leaders. The one she chooses can be based on subjective or objective rationale. The VP's decision may be influenced by other stakeholders, or she might decide based on who is more articulate, persuasive, or valuable.

Or, caught in a bind and not able to decipher who bears more of the responsibility for their power struggle, the VP may decide based purely on her personal affinity.

Shawn might have an unconscious bias toward Jada because they golf together, and after a few restless nights, she decides that her least painful option is to fire Martin. As word spreads throughout the organization, reactions will range from outrage and shock to relief and exhilaration. Martin's faction members are certain the organization will implode, but Jada's supporters are quietly thrilled.

Figure 4.7. "Unfortunately for you . . ."

Stage Nine: From afar and in the bar

I originally thought there were eight stages to escalated conflict. But working at a university, I discovered that the "Martins" of the world *don't* let go and go away.

Put yourself in Martin's shoes, and you'll see immediately that it would be almost impossible for him to accept his termination. The nightmare of the "social evaluation threat" has become his reality. Martin will continue to linger at the periphery of the organization. He will stay in contact with his former loyalists and hope that, with their help, he can discredit Jada. Martin hopes that Shawn will eventually realize she terminated *the wrong person.* He is intent in fanning the flames of discontent.

Martin and his entourage don't meet in a coffee shop or bowling alley. These small groups of disgruntled employees almost invariable meet in a bar—the perfect venue for negative speculation, ridicule of the target, and alcohol-fueled bonding. Energized by the terminated person's indignation, these alliances can continue for years. Unfortunately, most organizations are oblivious to these covert meetings and powerless to intervene.

Avoid these self-defeating mistakes

There is tremendous benefit to seeing the nine stages in print. As I mentioned at the onset of this chapter, there is dead silence when we cover this section in the seminar, because almost everyone has been caught up in a version of the nine stages sometime during their careers.

No one warned us about the hidden costs of faction building. No one said, "When you disagree, don't withdraw, don't vent, and don't build a group of loyalists at someone else's expense. These behaviors will destroy your reputation and your relationships; you will lose control over how this situation ends, and the fallout will interfere with your chances of promotion. You will be seen as someone who is willing to bankroll drama at the expense of solutions."

However, from here forward, we can all learn to avoid these common mistakes. We can commit to the absolute necessity of talking *to* people rather than *about* them.

In Chapter Ten, we'll explore a powerful template to accomplish this goal.

5

Stories that Stick

"We dance around in a ring and suppose
But the secret sits in the middle and knows."

—Robert Frost

Not all behavior is innocent. Addicts, con artists, and individuals with personality and character disorders are very real. Sometimes employees, presidents, or accountants *are* cooking the books. Laws are broken, innocents are victimized.

To protect themselves and hold individuals accountable, organizations wisely create policies and procedures, performance development systems, investigation protocols, drug testing, written reviews, audits, exit interviews, 360 feedback, EEOC policies, expense reports, inclusivity training, written warnings, and so on. If policies or laws are violated, organizations need to act.

The news is full of stories that involve fraud, mistreatment, and deception. However, the attention these dramatic accounts receive in the media often prevents us from seeing that often our worst fears are *not* realized.

Let's look at the numbers. I have successfully resolved more than 300 conflicts—some involved dozens of people. Only twice was the situation *not* related to misunderstandings and hidden realities.

In the other 290-plus situations, there was a "baby in the back seat," rather than malice, wholesale incompetence, or deceit. Consequently, I always enter conflict situations with the assumption that I am dealing with negative reciprocity, poor processes, lack of skill, system problems, or misperceptions. Until proven otherwise, I give people the benefit of the doubt, and it is seldom that they do not deserve it.

I have learned from experience to go down this path. However, most individuals don't have the advantage of seeing hundreds of conflicts through to resolution. Consequently, when a colleague or supervisor witnesses an individual behaving in irrational ways, most observers slip into First Assumption thinking.

The following stories illustrate the distorted realities that occur as individuals withdraw and speculate about the motives and reasons behind other people's behaviors. Perceptions based on speculation and assumptions are worse than useless. As we saw in Chapter Two, they become part of the problem because they draw others in to validate conclusions and feed indignation and fear. As individuals continue down the shaky pathway of negative assumptions, thinking becomes increasingly distorted.

The ubiquity of avoidance is truly a tragedy, because as the following stories show, once an individual learns the other party's hidden reasons, contempt usually transforms into compassion and a desire to connect.

The exasperated RN

A psychiatric nurse who attended a seminar came up to me on break and said, "Anna, your message is totally resonating with me. What you're saying reminds me of something I frequently experience at work. After I have a few days off and return to the unit, I look at the new patients standing in the halls or slouched in the lounge and think, 'Look at them! They are pathetic! Can't they shape up and at least take some pride in their appearance?'

"Then I go into the office for report. During the meeting nurses who are ending their shift update those of us who are coming on. By the time the previous shift has finished telling us the background of the new patients, I am humbled by the amount of trauma many have endured and I am embarrassed by my previous judgments.

"I go back on the ward, and my disgust has turned into respect and awe. I am amazed that many of these individuals are functioning at all, and impressed by their tenacity and will."

I have often thought about this nurse's words. They are a dramatic testimony to the fact that contempt is often the result of lack of information combined with negative speculation.

I have witnessed this many times when feuding parties come to the table and are stunned by the other party's hidden realities.

The shut-out employee

Several years ago I helped resolve a conflict between a supervisor, Joni, and her direct report, Ben. For several years, they had enjoyed a close working relationship and even attended each other's family weddings and graduations. However, during the six months prior to my arrival, they had withdrawn from each other. Both of them invested considerable energy in complaining to human resources and to Joni's boss about the other person's lack of cooperation. The HR director told me both individuals were feeling anxious, depressed, and mistreated.

In my interview with Ben, a fidgety, high-energy employee, he explained that their relationship began to deteriorate shortly after their organization moved into a new office building. At the time, Ben took several personal days to attend a family reunion. Unfortunately, his leave fell during the agency's busiest weeks. Ben feared that Joni, who had worked overtime to cover for Ben's time off, held his absence and his commitment to family against him. He knew that if this was correct, Joni was discriminating against him, but he feared he didn't have adequate evidence to prove his case.

In our interview, Ben told me that prior to the move he and Joni had shared an open workspace, but shortly after the move, Joni started to work with the door to her new office closed. Ben interpreted her new isolation as proof that she was becoming inaccessible and remote. As we know, there can be many possible reasons for her behavior. I encouraged Ben to inquire about her new habit the next time the three of us were together.

At our next meeting, Ben told Joni his fear that she had become aloof and withdrawn. He cited her closed door as "proof" of her unreasonable behavior. It was an astonishing moment. A look of disbelief flashed across Joni's face, and then she burst out laughing! Joni realized how ludicrous and distorted their standoff had become. She jumped up to show us what had actually happened.

Joni explained that when she moved into her new office, the door hung off plumb. When she arrived at work she would open the door and push it against the wall, but within a few minutes it would slowly swing half shut. She put in a maintenance report to have it fixed, but knew it would be added to the bottom of a long list of requests.

One morning, Joni opened her door, walked to her desk, picked up the papers she needed, turned around, and *pow!* Joni walked smack into the edge of the partially closed door. Rubbing her injured forehead, she decided to keep her door closed until maintenance could repair it. Unfortunately, this seemingly minor sequence of events happened at the same time Ben was feeling anxious about their relationship. He interpreted the closed door as proof that his supervisor was brooding about his inconvenient absence.

Ben had already taken the first steps of the nine stages of escalated conflict. First, he began to avoid Joni. Subsequently, his withdrawal limited the opportunities to find out the innocent reason behind Joni's behavior. Then through negative speculation, Ben started venting and recruiting support from his coworkers that Joni was an unreasonable, distant, and biased supervisor.

Joni noticed Ben's sudden coolness, and then more than one of Ben's coworkers told her about his campaign to discredit her reputation. Joni felt betrayed. Joni became increasingly more guarded in her interactions with Ben. As her warmth toward Ben waned, Ben interpreted her coolness as further evidence that his fears were correct. During the following weeks, they both continued to blame and obsess about the other person and enlist allies to support their views.

When I work with estranged employees, I first meet with each person alone to prepare an intensive, future-oriented conversation. Then the three of us sit down, and the two parties take turns presenting their concerns and reacting to each other's perceptions and requests. During our joint meeting, as Joni and Ben aired months of interpretations, assumptions, and speculations, the reasoning behind their behaviors became clear. By the end of our time together, it was clear that they could have avoided weeks of drama and angst if they had the courage and skills to talk to each other directly. This type of standoff—withdrawal, erroneous speculation, and recruitment of allies—occurs multiple times a day in almost all organizations.

Later in the book you'll learn to address sensitive issues in a way that is both safe and powerful. Never again will you have to worry what a person's behavior means. You will know how to open the dialogue and uncover the meaning behind other party's behaviors.

The missing supervisor

Sometimes the reason for puzzling behaviors turns out to be the opposite of what others assume.

I was working with an executive team at a high-tech manufacturing site when David, the VP of engineering, sought me out. He was at his wits' end over his lead supervisor's erratic behavior. Eddy had been a star performer for years, but lately he was coming to work looking haggard and unkempt. In addition, David was hearing complaints that Eddy had lengthy, unexplained absences from the floor.

Eddy's behavior was so enigmatic that rumors were circulating that he was using and perhaps dealing drugs. David began to fear the worst. He told me he had pleaded with Eddy, yelled at him, scolded him, and threatened to fire him. Nothing made a difference. Eddy remained tight-lipped about his absences, and his puzzling behavior continued without a satisfying explanation.

David was desperate to find a resolution to the situation and asked if I would talk to him. Although I felt a little pessimistic that I would learn anything new, I told David I was willing to give it a try.

When I sat down with Eddy in a private room, he was evasive and cocky. But after chatting a bit about his work and personal life, he began to relax. I told him his colleagues and boss were concerned about his uncharacteristic behavior, and they were speculating about the cause. David was worried because Eddy had been his rock. I asked Eddy if there was some way we could alleviate David's apprehension. I gently warned him that without a quick turnaround, David would be forced to take disciplinary action.

Eddy and I discussed different ways we could handle confidentiality, and eventually, Eddy confided, "I'm being treated for hepatitis B. I haven't told anyone because people associate hepatitis B with dirty needles and illegal drugs. I'm embarrassed. I acquired the illness from a blood transfusion, but still, I don't want my condition known because it will just start rumors. I am a lead supervisor and should set a good example.

"The doctor told me the medication, which lasts for months, would make me violently ill. He advised me to take sick leave, but we're short staffed, and I want to be here. I can handle it most days, but sometimes I'm so nauseous that I have to find a remote place to sit down and rest."

Eddy and I sat in silence for a few minutes. What had seemed like callous disregard for his crew and manager was really tenacious devotion. Eddy and I crafted a message for David that protected Eddy's privacy, but we were able to inform him that Eddy's absences from the floor had a legitimate cause, and would come to an end within a reasonable period of time.

When I met with David and shared the essence of what Eddy had told me, he was close to tears. I realized how deeply connected they were, and the depth of the respect and affection they had for each other was clear.

In public the two men were often crude toward each other, even a tad antagonistic, but when the chips were down, their commitment was unmistakable. Their mutual investment was evident in David's intense relief that Eddy would soon be back to his old self, and in Eddy's unwillingness to leave his boss shorthanded, despite his illness.

The brooding CEO

Peter was fairly late when he arrived at a public seminar. Then he spent the first ninety minutes oblivious to his surroundings. Instead of paying attention to what was going on in the session, he organized dozens of sticky notes in his calendar. Eventually, he finished his task, picked up his pen, and looked up. However, for the rest of the morning, he seemed only marginally attentive.

On break I learned that he was the CEO of a modest machine shop that was previously run by his father. Peter informed me that he had come to the seminar to learn something about conflict resolution, but he didn't say much more. I would learn later that he was truly a man of few words.

Two weeks after the seminar, Peter called me and asked if I'd give him feedback on a memo he had just written. I suspected that the memo was the tip of a very large iceberg, but I agreed to respond.

The memo was curt and to the point. Peter stated that shop employees started washing their hands *before* the bell rang for their fifteen-minute breaks. According to the memo, this was unacceptable, and the workers were to refrain immediately.

When Peter reached the end of the memo, he asked me what I thought. For a second I was tempted to assume there was something wrong with *Peter.* However, I canceled that thought and replaced it with an assumption that there must be a reason, a story, behind his odd behavior. I postponed giving my opinion of his memo and asked him a series of questions instead.

Peter had been CEO of the facility for six years. He had joined the company at his ailing father's urging, reluctantly leaving behind a lucrative job as CFO of another organization. At first, things had gone well; he started making improvements, and his rapport with the men had grown. But during contract negotiations, his forty-three shop workers unexpectedly went on strike.

After a three-week standoff, the workers settled and returned to work. However, Peter was furious. He started canceling the few simple pleasures that the crew had enjoyed for years. First he eliminated the doughnuts the company bought to celebrate birthdays. The next casualty was the company picnic. The letter he had just read to me was his third crackdown.

Peter was angry because every one of his contractions resulted in a pushback from the men, who matched his pettiness every step of the way. The workers prolonged smoke and bathroom breaks, ignored maintenance on the machines, and knowingly ran incorrect orders.

Without realizing it, Peter was engaged in the classic workplace power struggle where each side squares off, matches, and then "tops" the negative behavior of the other party. Behavior declines rapidly in these types of jostling matches. As we will see in Chapter Eight, reciprocity (the tendency to match another person's behavior for good or naught) is the most reliable predictor of human behavior.

At the end of our conversation I told Peter that, unfortunately, I didn't think his memo would help. I suggested that he and I work together to find the root cause of this standoff.

A few days later, I arrived at the plant. It was a run-down, dirty building filled with clutter and marred by neglect. Obviously no one paid much attention to working conditions. I would soon learn my assumption was dead wrong.

Peter took me on a tour. The further back we went into his facility, the more dilapidated the building became. In contrast to his fear that his workers were disloyal to him, I started getting the sense that they were one devoted, tenacious group of individuals who continued to show up for work despite the unpleasant working conditions.

After the tour, Peter gave me permission to interview eight of his crew individually and privately to hear their side of the story. One by one these proud and steadfast men sat on rickety stools in a barren office and told me why they were so unhappy.

When Peter's father had been president, the shop was like family to them. Over the years, they had found small but meaningful ways to take the tedium and monotony out of their day. They evolved into a gruff, tightly knit brotherhood.

However, since Peter had taken over, the financial health of the company had taken a significant downturn. There had been a freeze on salaries and pullbacks on benefits. After five years of stagnation, the men went on strike. When they settled the contract and returned to work they expected that Peter, like his father before him, would be standing at the door, welcoming them back and graciously relegating their tension to the past. Instead they discovered he had become a sullen, withdrawn, bitter man who cast a chill throughout the shop whenever he walked the floor.

The workers couldn't fathom his mood and resented his behavior. When they had gone on strike fifteen years earlier, the president had been pleased to see everyone back at work. The men felt they had exercised a legal right, played by the rules, and returned ready to make a go of it. Peter's behavior was unjust.

Only after I returned to Peter with a confidential (all the identifiers removed) summary of the operators' concerns did he reveal the rest of his story.

For the first time, his behavior made sense. I was humbled and touched by the hidden reality behind this quiet man. I learned what "baby" was hiding in the back seat.

However, if we were going to restore trust and communication, the rest of the crew needed to hear his rationale too. When I shared my reactions with Peter he agreed. The two of us hatched a plan.

The following week, Peter closed the plant at noon. Everyone gathered at the private dining room of a neighborhood restaurant that had been a place of celebration for company events in more affluent times. We shared a delicious (but uncomfortably quiet) meal, and when we finished, I asked the guys to help rearrange the furniture.

We put a table in the middle of the room, and the crew pulled their chairs in a circle around the table. Peter and his accountant sat on one side of the table, and across from them sat Steve, the union representative, and Lou, one of the more articulate operators.

After setting ground rules, I asked Steve and Lou to begin. I asked them to tell Peter what they had told me about how shocked they were about his recent behavior. The operator, union representative, and I had rehearsed their statement and it was respectful, void of assumptions, factual, and curious. True to his habits, Peter listened, but said very little.

Then it was Peter's turn. For the first time in their six years together, all forty-three shop workers saw a side of this enigmatic man that was unknown to them.

He talked about his early days at the shop, the camaraderie and friendly teasing he had enjoyed there as a kid, and how the experience had shaped his character and interests. For the first time he revealed the reluctance he felt about returning as CEO, and that his personal interests were overridden by a sense of duty to his father. Peter shared that his father would have had no retirement income if the plant closed.

Peter disclosed that the first thing he learned as CEO was that the economic repercussions from the first strike had been the reason his father never upgraded the facility. His father had owned a prime piece of property in an industrial park where he had planned to rebuild. However, after the first strike, his dad sold the land to make payroll.

When Peter became CEO, his long-term goal was to acquire enough equity to rebuild the crumbling facility. But he also learned that the company was precariously close to bankruptcy.

Throughout the next six years, Peter used every strategy he knew as a former CFO to turn the company around. He was nearing his goal and was preparing a mortgage application when the union president told him the men had voted to strike. His dream, and six years of struggles, went up in smoke.

Peter knew the loan officer would ask two questions: "Do you have a union?" and "Have they ever been on strike?" He knew that if he answered yes to the second question, his chances of getting a loan would vanish. Without a modern facility and new equipment, Peter knew the company would continue to struggle.

When he received the call from the union president, Peter felt betrayed that the crew had not done what they had in previous years: refuse the contract but continue to work.

As Peter explained the reasons for his frustration and disappointment, the room became totally still. The crew's anger and indignation were gone. What had previously seemed like his selfishness and brooding callousness was really unfailing devotion to the business.

Steve, the union representative, respectfully explained to Peter why they had made their decision. The operators had met on a Friday night to vote on the contract. The union president gave them two choices: either accept the contract or go on strike. It was Steve's first year as their company's union representative, and he was too green to realize they had a third option: to return to work without a signed contract and continue to negotiate. He took the union president at his word and encouraged the members to strike. Of course, the employees had no idea what was at stake.

The conversation in the restaurant was the first time they heard each other's reasoning. Everyone slouched in their chairs. The enemy evaporated. What remained was misconstrued loyalty, misunderstanding, and the tremendous sense of loss that comes when one realizes that their self-righteousness was not only unwarranted but had become the biggest barrier to resolution.

We took a break while everyone regrouped intellectually and emotionally. When they came back, we spent the next two hours brainstorming how Peter and the operators could address the chronic issues they needed to resolve in order to optimize their chances of success. For the first time in months, they were working together as a team.

I stayed in touch with Peter during the next few weeks, and then checked in every year or so, just to see how things were going. Together, his company created process improvement teams, and relationships between management and operators were at an all-time high. Peter's voice reflected the joy of working together in alignment, despite tremendous odds. Later he sent me a letter: "Thank you. You saved the relationships and probably the company."

As these stories show, when we face frustration, we make an assumption. Either our aggravation is caused by someone's incompetence, our own idiocy, or there's a pressing constraint or pressure hidden from view.

When we move to the third option, we become curious, and only then are we emotionally primed to reach out and begin a conversation—perhaps the very conversation that will save your company or team.

6

The Invisible Costs of Contempt

"If you judge people, you have no time to love them."
—Mother Theresa

As we have established, the immediate payoffs of First Assumption are a sugar high, self-righteous indignation, and the superficial sense that we are elevating our status and bonding.

Unfortunately, the costs are hidden and delayed. Even though my work is immersed in workplace conflict, it took me many years to realize the costs of contempt.

Previously, we covered the four disadvantages of First Assumption:

1. The risk of depression.
2. The inability to think clearly, comprehend what is being said, and recall what happens when we flood.
3. Flooding is a risk for heart disease.
4. The loss of positive energy and camaraderie.

Following are ten additional costs. Knowing how these mistakes have damaged the prospects of others motivates us to be disciplined when we react to frustration and disagreement.

Cost 1: Mind-boggling amounts of wasted money

After we shift from First to Third Assumptions, many of my clients skillfully cover up their embarrassment as they painlessly solve entrenched problems that have festered in the background for months or even years.

The real problems, which are typically systemic, have been draining millions of hard-earned dollars while leaders and employees have been distracted by factions and drama. When organizations focus on people, problems are covered up, excused, and downplayed, or conversely, exaggerated and distorted. In the meantime, good citizen behaviors such as objective fact-finding, acknowledgement of other's contributions, admitting an oversight, collaborating, lending a hand, and side-by-side problem-solving have all but disappeared.

It's impossible to address the real causes of tension and waste when the key players are involved in a high-stakes power struggle. None of these costs are tracked or analyzed, and yet these power struggles are everywhere. In Chapter Nine, we'll drill down into a case study to get a sense of how much these dramas cost.

Cost 2: Problems multiply

When individuals avoid each other, the best-case scenario is the decisions for which they are responsible are delayed. In other situations, decisions are made without the input of key stakeholders, and quality is compromised. Frequently, decisions are simply abandoned and colleagues and employees stumble without direction. In the worst scenarios, decisions become weapons with the explicit intent to undermine an adversary and diminish their success.

When families did their own mending, there was a saying: "A stitch in time saves nine." But during escalated conflict, the opposite has happened. The entire hem has fallen to the floor and everyone is tripping over it. Workplaces are so complex and interdependent that when one entity falters, the ripple spreads throughout the organization.

In conflict resolution projects, there is always a point at which parties have acquired enough rapport and trust that we can shift our focus to backlogged decisions. I am impressed and relieved when the talent and expertise of my clients rises to the surface again and they begin to identify solutions. They had the ability to reach these agreements, but during escalated conflict, solutions slipped through their fingers

I worked with a senior executive at a food bank on the east coast. He and his direct report were estranged, and after he heard me speak at a conference, he asked for my help. Prior to my arrival, their human resource representative tried to facilitate a resolution meeting between the two, which ended in a shouting match that was heard throughout the building. Their conflict included every dynamic that we've covered thus far in this book. After working together for a day and a half, the director said to me, "After we took out the drama, it was just logistics, wasn't it?"

Cost 3: Partners in crime sell each other down the river

Betrayal is the biggest risk of First Assumption. Colleagues and direct reports can take denigrating comments directly to the targeted person. I saw this behavior clip the rising career of a brilliant professional without any awareness on his part.

A university human resource professional asked me to untangle a conflict. One of the professors, Adam, had been at the school for many years. He was quiet, withdrawn, and his social skills needed polish. However, Adam's work was consistent and reliable.

Three years before my arrival, his colleague, Lance, who was gregarious, charming, and a recent PhD graduate of an ivy league school joined the university after being recruited aggressively. The institution hoped to benefit from Lance's prestigious reputation.

Adam had applied for the position Lance acquired, and Lance soon felt his resentment. Lance fell back on a now familiar strategy of bonding with Adam by nurturing a deep dislike for the dean, Pamela. Their obsession was so intense that every morning, they would shut themselves in Lance's office for coffee, doughnuts, and the daily round of "Pummeling Pamela." They denigrated her decisions, her academic background, and her looks.

However, during Lance's third year, Adam made a series of errors. At first, Lance hid his colleague's mistakes, but eventually Pamela discovered this scheme. She was furious and insisted that Lance give Adam a written warning.

Adam, who was used to being a respected, albeit modest, performer handled his fall from grace poorly. He withdrew even further from the social life of the office and the quality of his work deteriorated. Increasingly, the high-status assignments were handled by Lance.

Several months into this painful decline, Adam made a desperate attempt to regain some of his status by tarnishing Lance's rising star. Unfortunately, Lance had given Adam plenty of ammunition to accomplish his goal.

Adam stopped by Pamela's office and asked if he could share something in confidence. Pamela agreed, and Adam disclosed some of the most noxious comments Lance had made behind her back. To boost his credibility, he included insider information that Pamela had told Lance in confidence, which Adam could not have learned from anyone else.

Despite the fact that Adam's self-oriented motives were transparent, he achieved his goal. Pamela agreed to confidentiality before her conversation. Consequently, she decided not to confront Lance directly. Instead, she retaliated subtly, and quietly blocked future advancements.

Lance continued to work at the school, oblivious to the fact that his colleague, Adam, had poisoned his relationship with the person who had the most influence over his future. Lance had unwittingly played a significant role in his own downfall by choosing to bond with Adam by creating an adversarial faction against Pamela.

Although this was the most extreme act of betrayal I have witnessed, I have seen many that are less dramatic. These situations have taught me that the only way we can keep others from repeating our disparaging comments is to never give them material to exploit. Refusing to initiate or take part in backstabbing not only preserves our reputations for integrity and honesty, but it's also essential to maintain a clean and unabashed relationship with anyone who affects our careers.

Once we target another person, our relationship begins to change. We can never be certain if they have heard our disparaging remarks, and that subtle doubt will affect our interactions. We will become slightly more guarded, less warm, and uneasy in their presence. A shift that they often detect and reciprocate.

If we are not willing to make a comment directly to a colleague, we should refrain from saying it to someone else, no matter how clever or witty we think we are. It's too likely that it will be relayed to the target—and because we will not be informed, we will be powerless to undo the harm.

During my time at this organization, it was so clear to me that Lance could have moved in the opposite direction. When he sensed Adam's resentment, he could have become invested in his well-being and found ways to advocate for him and help him advance.

In a sense, Lance's mistakes are our gains because we can learn from his experience. But if I had had a reset button for him, I surely would have pushed it.

Cost 4: Credibility suffers

Sometimes people use First Assumption to sidestep responsibility. Individuals hope that by pointing a finger their own behavior won't be scrutinized.

However, the "Quick! Look over there!" scapegoat strategy harms, rather than helps, our reputations and careers. Colleagues, supervisors, and direct reports learn to doubt our word and suspect, fairly or not, that our version of truth is likely to be incomplete or distorted.

If I attempt to convince my supervisor, Larry, that the cause of a joint problem lies entirely within someone else's domain and I am merely an innocent bystander, it will not be long before he gathers enough information to discover that I am covering up my role in the problem.

However, it is unlikely that Larry will mention his findings to me. He will anticipate more denials, and he won't want to waste his time. Consequently, I will not discover how his opinion of me plummeted when he uncovered facts I withheld. Larry will surmise that he cannot take me at my word, and will resent having to fact-find on his own, rather than trust me to relay the situation accurately.

Cost 5: Resentment of First Assumption leaders and colleagues

Direct reports and colleagues carry deep, carefully hidden resentments when a supervisor attempts to discredit others as a means of winning allies. They won't speak up for one very heartbreaking reason: they do not want to become the next target. *Everyone* pays a price for First Assumption.

This happened at a respected high-tech R&D company. They were conducting small-scale experiments on new applications of rare minerals. Rob, the director of operations, ridiculed the chief engineer with the regularity of an atomic clock. When Rob was present, the operators would grin and shrug as he spun his latest "evidence" of the engineer's incompetence.

However, in private interviews, every one of the seven operators told me, "I wish Rob would stop. It's like he *wants* the engineers to fail. Sometimes I think he sets them up. Rob is making our jobs harder—not easier."

When I shared this feedback with Rob, he was astonished. By pointing out the foibles in the engineering department, he thought he was elevating himself and his team. But his direct reports were correct; he was making their jobs more difficult.

When it was time for Rob to share his feedback with his team, he had the courage to admit his mistake to his direct reports, apologize, and commit to ending his daily ritual of disrespecting the engineers. We created a feedback loop by giving his direct reports permission to speak up if he broke his commitment.

When the boss targets others, few direct reports confront the situation directly. However, as the following story reveals, resentment simmers just below the surface.

The troubled dialysis unit

I have clear memories of sitting in my small office at a major metropolitan hospital when a vice president, Eleanor, whipped in and plopped down in a seat next to my desk. I was a recent graduate, a newly licensed psychologist, and an organizational development consultant with one year of experience. Pretty green.

Eleanor was usually laid back and funny, but at this moment, she was dead serious. "Anna, there's an escalated conflict in our dialysis unit. There are three leaders in this unit: the head nurse, the assistant head nurse, and the head of the "techs," the group that services the dialysis machines.

"They are embroiled in a fight that has drawn in other employees and is widely known throughout the hospital. Nurses tell me privately that everyone has picked a side, and the preoccupation with the conflict is compromising patient safety. Even the patients hear stories about this drama! I'm going to close down the dialysis unit and send patients to another hospital if you don't go up there and fix it."

Me? I remember three simultaneous realizations:

1. Her duty to protect patient safety would mean revenue loss that would run into the millions.
2. Despite two degrees and years of training in psychology, I had no idea what to do.
3. If I lacked skills in conflict resolution, probably most employees did, too. Where else in the hospital could Eleanor go?

Regardless, I had no plan and no process, so I jumped right in and flew by the seat of my pants.

I asked to speak to each of the three leaders alone. They each had different versions of the situation, but individually they had come to the same conclusion: Each of the three leaders believed they were winning. In private interviews they told me *they* had the majority of staff loyalty and respect.

Obviously, they were deluded. But how could I break through their illusions in a way that would not make them defensive? I asked them if they would agree to an anonymous employee survey. They all readily agreed because they were each confident that *they* were the hero of the staff narrative.

You, dear reader, can anticipate the outcome more accurately than they did. As you have probably guessed, the feedback on *all three* was extremely critical and occasionally crude. The staff comments were laced with bitter complaints about the immaturity and irresponsibility of the three leaders. In contrast to the leaders' beliefs that they were winning staff loyalty, the staff was furious at the leadership group for destroying the unit's cohesiveness in order to fulfill their personal vendettas.

After removing all identifying information, I turned their data into a master document, asked the three of them to join me in a small meeting room, and gave them each a copy. To say I felt anxious about their reactions is inaccurate. I was terrified (and I would handle this situation differently today). But the ad hoc process worked. There was silence in the room, throat clearing, paging and re-paging through data, tight jaws, and eyes everywhere but on each other.

But here is the lesson that we landed on that day: the goal of each individual had been to save their reputation by obliterating the status of the other two. They each had the same goal: to get the others demoted, fired, sent to the corner facing the wall.

Now their secrets were exposed, and they realized they had covertly shared the same false hope. However, even if they succeeded in getting one or both of their colleagues fired, they would not have "won." The controversy would have roiled on. As we covered in "The Nine Stages of Escalated Conflict," loyalists to a terminated leader guarantee the team does not heal, and their workplace continues to be full of tension and drama.

Together the four of us contemplated the reality that the only way they could salvage their reputations in the hospital was together. Their hostility toward each began to soften, and small overtures of reconciliation occurred. That afternoon we began the hard dig to the root causes of, and solutions to, their disagreements. They eventually apologized to the staff for their disruptive feud and returned to reputable leadership based on client needs. Their reconciliation lasted for several years until, one by one, they left for opportunities at other medical centers. However, they left with their reputations and futures intact.

Since those early days, I've seen many similar scenarios in which individuals believe that escalation and dominance, including the obliteration of the other person's status, are the only way out of escalated conflict.

However, as you proceed through these pages, you'll discover that there's a better way. You'll discover how to back away from the free fall of escalated conflict and never again find yourself feeling like you have to "win."

Cost 6: Blame turns potential allies into enemies

As the following story reveals, power struggles alienate individuals who are, or could become, significant assets to our careers.

The president's torn loyalties

The president of a high-tech printing company asked for assistance with a conflict between the "two most important people in my life." The VP of sales, Mark, was the president's son, a dapper, polished young man and proud recipient of a newly acquired MBA. The president's business partner of thirty years, Bob, was the COO, and he was an easygoing, reliable, salt-of-the-earth graduate from the school of hard knocks.

These two executives couldn't have been more different in upbringing and outlook. When I arrived at the company, their disagreements about the future direction of the organization had been simmering for two years. Mark and Bob were each accumulating evidence and privately lobbying the president to terminate the other person.

At the height of the conflict, Mark had reluctantly invited Bob to a sales meeting at the offices of one of their biggest customers. Because Bob had years of experience with the technicalities of their products and Mark was relatively new to the trade, Mark needed Bob's expertise to close the deal.

However, Mark's desire to see his nemesis fail couldn't help but impact the meeting. Mark neglected to coach Bob on the norms and formality of a high-status meeting. Bob, who had never been included in a sophisticated sales call, arrived in scruffy attire that was appropriate for the shop floor, but not a corporate environment.

Bob's embarrassment and discomfort over his obvious faux paus increased as the meeting progressed. Bob was in over his head and didn't know how to regain his equilibrium. Unfortunately, he fell back on a technique that worked well back at the plant: he swore. In this setting, however, his language hung awkwardly in the air, and the meeting came to a premature end. No more than five minutes after returning to work, Mark was in his father's office with the latest proof that Bob was too old-school and clumsy to make the transition to working with high-end corporate clients.

However, Bob had his own ways to bring Mark down. He deftly undermined Mark's support and popularity. With his crew—the majority of the employees—Bob spread accusations that Mark was a hopeless, silver-spoon opportunist totally out of touch with the realities of their trade and privileged only by his father's authority. Consequently, when Mark walked the shop floor, the crew would barely acknowledge his presence, let alone help him learn the nuances of the trade.

Although the conflict centered on these two men, every employee in the organization knew about this conflict, fed it, gossiped about it, and picked sides.

Employees in their respective departments carried half-baked prejudices and unjust criticisms of both leaders, and eventually everyone in their departments. Customers were pulled into the web. The two men became invested in the other's decline and began contributing to each other's blunders. It undoubtedly cost the organization thousands, if not millions, of unmeasured dollars in the form of off-task behavior, lost opportunities, and deep mistrust between operations and sales.

The hapless father/owner responded to the tension and his torn loyalties in a manner similar to many conflicted leaders: he spent more time at the golf course! The organization's growth was stymied, and system problems grew.

I worked with Mark and Bob intermittently over several weeks. As they began to learn more about each other and address the root causes of their disagreements, they realized the vast majority of their dislike and fear was based on rumors and speculations that were distorted and amplified as they circulated through the organization.

Now, face to face, they talked in-depth about their expertise, ideas for expansion, and their vision of the future. Their commitment to the company and its owner was obvious, even though it was expressed in very different ways. Bob showed his devotion through his unwavering reliability and know-how. Mark's commitment to his father's enterprise was expressed through gutsy and charismatic risk-taking. During the time we met, their annoyance developed into admiration. Their former hostility over the dramatic differences in their personalities morphed into fascination over the unique combination of Bob's superb craftsmanship and Mark's creativity, chutzpah, and business savvy.

As their bond solidified, they knew they had to break the habit of bringing forward distorted half-truths and speculations about the other person. I suggested they not only tell other employees that they had begun to strengthen and repair their partnership but also to begin speaking highly of each other in front of their direct reports, peers, and the president. The message was out. The conflict between the two men was history and employees gratefully dropped their guard and settled back into work.

I enjoyed several meetings with the executive team over the next few months and watched Bob and Mark become each other's strongest defenders. On multiple occasions, I observed one or the other spontaneously come to the other's defense. I stayed in touch and learned that the company entered new markets and created products that revitalized the organization.

At the close of the project, the president struggled to express his profound relief that the tension between the two most important people in his life had finally come to an end. He had been painfully caught in the middle, feeling guilty and disloyal. I suspect that the resolution of Bob and Mark's conflict not only contributed to the prosperity of the company but it also added several years to the president's life.

Sometimes when I dig for the original barriers to a working alliance, all I find are fragments of rumors and negative speculations. It makes me wonder how many brilliant partnerships have crumbled under the paradoxical weight that the vacuum between two key players creates.

Cost 7: Blame becomes an automatic response

Sometimes individuals with low interpersonal skills or poor self-confidence compensate for insecurities by tearing others down. Sadly, sarcasm and putdowns become the one thing at which they excel, and they use it to increase their status within the group. They often develop a cutting sense of humor and a keen ability to deflate the intentions of any person or project. The quip in mental health circles is that "hurt people, hurt people."

Repetition strengthens neurons, and denigrating remarks can easily become an automatic response. We read about sports figures who are unable to stop destructive, aggressive reactions even when faced with the loss of their jobs. And we've seen politicians whose use of First Assumption was the undoing of their political careers. Early in a campaign, voters may admire their irreverent style and willingness to challenge the status quo. However, as their term progresses, their aggressive reactions fail to bring about substantive solutions, they alienate the press and their colleagues, and eventually, their broad base of support.

Cost 8: Blame demoralizes employees and destroys pride in work

Leaders are conduits of information. Explaining the rationale behind management decisions is one of their most important roles. This does not mean they need to agree with every decision. Leaders at all levels need to be involved in ongoing dialogue and share their enthusiasm and doubts about decisions. However, there is a world of difference between face-to-face disagreement and ridiculing other decision makers behind their backs. Denigrating other leaders destroys employees' motivation, morale, and pride in work.

Conflict within the ranks

Until I worked with chiefs of police and supervisors, I didn't clearly see the link between First Assumption and the loss of pride in work.

The first time I facilitated a seminar with a police department, I was somewhat paranoid. Leaving home, I kept checking my driver's license, car tabs, and insurance card. A room full of constabularies! Despite my nervousness, the officers were warm, funny, and grateful to learn about flooding, heart disease, and hostility.

What surprised me most was that they all agreed that interacting with perpetrators or victims was *not* the hardest part of their jobs. In a group of eighty officers there was a strong consensus that the most demoralizing part of their work was conflict *within the ranks.*

Midmorning during the seminar, three officers were paged out of the room. A local citizen had locked himself in his apartment with an arsenal of guns, threatening to kill himself or anyone else within range. My heart went out to the officers as they left. I learned later that they convinced the man to surrender, and he was taken to jail for a psychological evaluation.

That evening as I drove back to the Twin Cities, the incident triggered a stream of questions. I wondered what it would be like to have a job in which you risked your life and reported to a boss who used First Assumption.

Imagine Trevon, a seasoned officer, returning from this dangerous call. In his situation, it would be appropriate for the officer, who minutes ago risked his life, to be flooded with adrenaline, cortisol, and hormones. Because of the fight-or-flight response, his blood would have thickened to prevent blood loss, and his pulse and blood pressure would be elevated.

Consequently, Trevon, who is partially (and appropriately) flooded, is primed to overreact to the next frustration. Sure enough, he sees an email from the mayor, Joy. The email begins, "I regret to inform you that your department's request for upgraded bulletproof vests has been denied."

He marches into the chief's office and demands, "Have you seen this? What an idiot! Does the mayor know anything about police work? Has she ever walked a beat? All she cares about getting re-elected, like all politicians!"

This is a critical moment for the chief. If he takes the bait, his reflexive response will be similar to: "I saw that memo. I'm convinced Joy is depriving some village of an idiot. If you think that's bad, wait until I tell you what she said at the team-building barbeque when she didn't think I could hear her."

If the officer and chief continue down this path they will address the problem with First Assumption. They are primed for attack and withdraw—and they will probably do both.

If they attack the mayor by spreading negative opinions of her, it is unlikely they will be in a mind set to problem solve with her. After they agree she is a political sell-out, there is little chance they'll be successful in changing her mind.

There's a consequence to this conversation that will occur after the meeting that most leaders miss. Although the supervisor has superficially bonded with the officer, his behavior has failed to bridge him to the upper management and the mission of the department.

After Trevon leaves his supervisor's office, he has to go back on his beat. Halfway to his squad car, it will hit him: "Wait a minute. I'm putting my life on the line for a self-serving political has-been! I'm a chump! Why do I care so much about this place? I think I'll call in sick."

After multiple repetitions of this scenario with various officers, the chief will discover that he has a demoralized workforce. He will sense that his officers' pride is waning, or they are becoming increasingly fixated on the financial aspects of their work. Without knowing it, the chief is inadvertently destroying the intrinsic rewards of work, which include service, pride, camaraderie, identity, and meaning.

Employees want their sacrifices, overtime, and commitment to matter. When they are told their leaders are incompetent or unethical, they feel foolish for caring.

When the chief uses ridicule to explain disappointments, he lowers the possibility that staff will understand the pressures and opportunities of their organization and leverage its strengths. Without information employees cannot align their efforts in a meaningful way, nor will they feel pride in belonging to an ethical workplace worthy of their deep investments.

When leaders attribute the source of a problem to people, it means *they* must change in order for the problem to be resolved. This is unlikely, so employees will conclude that they are stuck with intractable problems, and their desire to improve and make a deep commitment to work will decrease.

Cost 9: We risk being seen as hypocrites

Returning to the previous example of the chief and his officer, imagine that after they've done a thorough job of discrediting Joy, she unexpectedly drops in. The chief quickly shifts gears and responds to his supervisor with warmth and a statement that he is pleasantly surprised to see her. They start sharing insider stories about the barbeque cook-off and who might have been too friendly with the judges.

While the chief retreats from his negative behaviors from just moments ago and chats up the mayor, the officer is busy "reading" the chief.

The officer won't miss a single nuance. He concludes that the chief is a hypocrite willing to flatter and charm the same people he ridiculed just seconds ago.

The officer wonders whether the chief does the same thing behind *his* back. The officer never again feels certain that his supervisor speaks well of him in his absence, or will come to his defense.

Even if Trevon previously looked up to the chief, he now sees him as a blowhard without a moral compass.

Cost 10: Accountability and standards decline

Employees and leaders go above and beyond because they have pride in what they do and the mission of the organization. However, after the chief denigrates the leadership of the organization, he is going to have a hard time holding Trevon accountable.

Trevon has become disillusioned with the department and its leadership. Later when he sees his colleagues at the union meeting, he'll share what he witnessed, and disenchantment will spread.

No one is safe

Blame is on the rise in our society. Conservatives blame liberals, liberals blame neoconservatives, parents blame schools, schools blame society, the rich blame the poor, the poor blame the 1 percent. Wives blame husbands, husbands blame the boss, farmers blame immigrants, and corporations blame government. We blame based on race, religion, ethnicity, gender, political leaning, sexual orientation, and age. We blame politicians, minorities, the police, attorneys, and so on. Any perceivable difference will do.

I have seen groups break into coalitions based on the kind of motorcycle they drove to work or the sports team they favored. Workplaces divide into destructive factions based on age, education, union membership, shift, rank, geographic location, longevity, gender, race, and job function.

When we use First Assumption, we signal to others that we tolerate blame. Eventually, they will turn the arrow of contempt in our direction. After all, we taught them that denigrating others is an appropriate response.

In the next chapter, we will cover a powerful alternative to blame when a colleague or customer is flooded. Using the following technique we will see how to save relationships, bond with direct reports, *and address the problem!* If we avoid the mistakes of the chief, we will be able to preserve morale and protect our reputations as individuals with integrity.

7

Strategies for Calming Others, Calming Self

"One kind word warms
three winter months."
—Japanese proverb

The world can feel crowded, demanding, and impersonal. Consequently, strategies to refuel and calm our bodies are essential. In this chapter, we will cover specific techniques that replace reflexive reactions (blame others, blame self) with responses that are more useful and effective.

We have already covered the basics of why you should make this life-altering change. You have learned about First, Second, and Third Assumptions; baby in the back seat; the negativity bias of the brain; flooding; heart disease; the thinking pattern associated with depression; the conditions and biochemicals of connection; inflammatory thinking; the helper's high; post-traumatic growth; drama-venting; the nine stages of escalated conflict; adversarial factions; the hidden costs of contempt; and the link between cynicism, hostility, and low self-esteem,

Now let's turn our attention to some of the strategies that make change possible. First, we'll piggyback off the story of the chief and officer, and see how the chief could have bonded with his employee, maintained his integrity, *and* solved the problem. I will share a template (EASE) I've used dozens of times for calming down a flooded colleague, customer, or family member.

Second, we'll look at how *we* can stop flooding. There is an abundance of techniques, but I'm going to limit our focus to the ones I found most effective.

Third, we will address changes in our personal lives that support a shift from unhealthy to healthy patterns. Again, it does not work to just stop flooding. That strategy leaves us with no energy, and that is the condition we hate the most. To maintain our gains we must replace hostility with activities and people who sustain our growth.

There are two caveats before we jump into the next technique, EASE. This strategy isn't appropriate if you feel physically threatened. Then it is time to exit or call for help. However, except for extraordinary situations, the anger we face in the workplace isn't physical; it is verbal and emotional.

I also want to share one simple strategy that works *if* the other person understands the concept of flooding. In both my professional and personal life, I've said to someone who is flooding, "You are being a bit aggressive, and now *I* am starting to flood. Can you give me fifteen minutes to regain my equilibrium, and then we can try again? I want to give you an answer that is well thought through and works for both of us." When I use this response and make it about me, not them, the other person apologizes!

In the beginning of your transition to Third Assumption and blame-free thinking, your cronies and colleagues may still invite you to join them in denigrating another person or group. If you have been prone to blaming others in the past, there will be moments when others will expect you to ridicule a well-worn scapegoat, and they may be surprised if you no longer join in.

You can tell people directly that you made a decision to stop engaging in labeling, inflammatory thinking, and targeting others. Tell them your cardiologist insisted!

Many attendees have told me that after attending the seminar they conducted mini-seminars with their family and colleagues, explained the three thinking patterns, baby in the back seat, and flooding. One attendee told me that soon after he shared the material with his children, they started saying, "Daddy, don't flood."

If you prefer, you can make the transition so seamless and effortless that others won't even notice that you no longer join in when a group starts ridiculing a favorite target. Your supervisor, colleagues, and direct reports may be puzzled when you seem less reactive and more analytical, but most likely they will not be able to pinpoint the exact nature of your change.

EASE: empathy, appreciation, search for solutions, explore

We can quickly see the advantages of sidestepping an invitation to blame someone by returning to the situation of the police officer from the previous chapter. That scenario is a perfect example of a direct report setting up his supervisor to blame the boss's boss. How naughty, and yet simultaneously delicious!

A quick summary of the facts: three officers were paged out of a seminar to respond to a resident who had barricaded himself in an apartment with a small arsenal of guns. With great skill and courage, the officers convinced the gunman to surrender.

As we build on this story, we imagine one of the officers returning to his desk and finding an email from the mayor that denies the chief's request for upgraded bulletproof vests. The officer, who is still dealing with the after effects of a high-risk situation, sees the memo, floods again, and storms into his chief's office to blast the mayor.

In our original scenario, the chief does everything wrong. He surrenders to the temptation of attributing the department's problems to someone who is not in the room and targets the mayor, which results in an abundance of hidden costs. The chief reacted reflexively to his officer's frustration, and he paid a price for his behavior. It's in our best interests to have a plan for these situations.

How do we calm someone who is flooded? In the following template, we'll see how the chief can calm and bond with his officer, preserve his pride in the organization, and move closer to his goal. This is Third Assumption at its best.

I named this strategy "EASE" because each letter stands for a step in the process. The technique utilizes the same principles that Michael and Julie Weisser used intuitively when they defused the anger of Larry Trapp, the KKK's grand dragon. In a sense, this is a hardheaded search for solutions combined with warmth and appreciation. As Larry discovered, even he was unable to resist this approach.

When you use this technique with someone who is flooded, he or she will drop the energy of negativity in a heartbeat for a chance to feel the calming energy of genuine appreciation.

There are four steps to EASE: empathy, appreciation, search for solutions, and explore.

First we'll apply EASE to the chief's situation, then we'll shift and give you an opportunity to respond to a situation you would like to improve.

1. Be empathic to the speaker's frustration

Empathy does not mean we have to agree with a frustrated speaker, although we may. Genuine empathy requires feeling another person's expressed and unexpressed emotions.

Let's return to Trevon, the officer from the previous chapter. The first step takes discipline because it requires that we pay attention to what he is saying. We cannot rehearse our pushback or our own grievances about the targeted person and expect to respond to Trevon's frustration effectively. We need to quickly size up the essence of his distress. The more we get in his shoes and accurately understand his perspective, the more he will calm down and listen when we summarize the reason for his anger. Connecting is calming.

Trevon will become more agitated and aggressive if he feels his concerns have been dismissed ("You don't have it so bad!") or minimized ("It could be worse. The county is down two sheriffs. Quit complaining!"). Listening to the exact nature of Trevon's discomfort and seeking to understand his frustration bonds the speaker and the listener.

Imagine *you* are the chief of police and Trevon has returned from the dangerous assignment. He is justifiably frustrated about finding an email that denies the upgraded safety equipment. We can help him manage his anger if we acknowledge his frustration.

First, the chief should react to the reality of the officer's situation. He can acknowledge that returning from a dangerous run and finding the email is infuriating. The chief can understand that the officer's reaction makes sense. Trevon is having strong, negative reactions because he fears his safety is not a priority.

If you were the chief, what would be *your* opening statement?

2. State your appreciation for his or her commitment, expertise, and efforts

Helping a colleague or customer shift their physiology of anger to the energy of appreciation is one of the most effective ways to alleviate the discomfort that accompanies flooding. This approach requires both knowledge about the person's behavior and having an open heart. If we are not *feeling* empathy and appreciation for the human being seated before us, we will not be effective.

Often, when individuals flood, it is because they don't feel valued or acknowledged. In step two, speak directly to the heart of the issue and give Trevon what he craves: respect for the sacrifices he makes every day that are overlooked or taken for granted. The chief can shift the emotional tone of the conversation by acknowledging the depth of Trevon's commitment to the city, his skills, or courage in handling the dangerous situation to which he responded.

When I use this approach, individuals drop their hostility. They listen intently and start to relax. The key is skillfully recognizing their intentions, contributions, and perhaps disappointment or hurt that their commitment or skill is being overlooked. You may remember that Barbara Fredrickson in *Love 2.0* calls connection "sustenance."

The chief could ask for details about how they disarmed the resident or acknowledge and commend his officers' expertise in handling the incident. Trevon and his fellow officers convinced a resident to surrender—an act that took tremendous skill.

If you were Trevon's supervisor, how would you express your appreciation? What could he say that might motivate Trevon to drop his anger in exchange for the opportunity to hear someone pay tribute to his commitment, service, and professionalism?

3. Speculate about reasons

Trevon is starting to drop his hostility. His shift to Third Assumption will be complete if the chief starts speculating about the mayor or city council's rationale. What "baby" might they have in the back seat?

The chief can take this step even if he does not know the reason or agree with the city council's conclusion. At this juncture, it is important that the chief takes the focus off the mayor's personality and puts it solidly on the situation. The options are limitless. Perhaps the city council is facing a budget shortfall. Possibly they are misinformed about the efficacy of the existing vests. How would you segue the officer from thinking that the problem is incompetent leadership to brainstorming what was behind the mayor and city council's decision?

4. Explore next steps

When the chief addresses the situation in this manner, he has acknowledged that there is a problem and has bonded with his direct report *without* incriminating the mayor. Now, the chief can identify a specific, measurable next step.

The fourth step is reassuring to a direct report. It's clear the supervisor is more than talk. In most cases, direct reports have no choice but to rely on their supervisor's willingness to act on problems that are important to frontline employees.

The chief could make several suggestions. Perhaps they need to find research about the effectiveness of the existing vests. They could invite the mayor to their next staff meeting to discuss options and barriers or the chief could simply pick up his phone. The chief could invite the officer to a meeting with the mayor so she can hear firsthand how this issue affects morale. Or maybe the chief already knows why the situation is not worth pursuing with the city, and they need to start looking for alternative sources of funding.

Again, take a few minutes to imagine and note a reasonable next step for the chief and his officer.

If we want to eliminate the hazards of blame from our lives, our ability to connect with our colleagues and customers when they're frustrated is critical. I think this is the meaning of the latter half of Einstein's quote in Chapter One, "It takes a touch of genius and a lot of courage to move in the opposite direction." Emotionally we cannot sit on the sidelines and expect to connect with our colleagues or direct reports at work. We have to step up, take a risk, and become *vulnerable.*

Calming a colleague or direct report

Following is an opportunity to apply these insights to a situation in your life. Identify an ongoing frustration for you, your direct reports, colleagues, or customers that often results in someone storming into your work area flooded and intent on "drama-venting." Identify an ongoing frustration and the person or group who typically gets blamed.

1. Empathy

Imagine a colleague interrupts your morning to vent over a leader's behavior. What's a common complaint? How could you bond through the use of empathy—a stated understanding of the frustrations the other person is feeling?

Again, listen for the hurt and wounded pride under anger. Do this without agreeing that the cause of their frustration is a person, department, or group. Acknowledging the speaker's frustration with warmth and understanding is enough to bond.

2. Appreciation

Write a statement or two to appreciate the person and his or her efforts.

You might comment on the speaker's level of expertise, their desire to resolve the situation, the investment they have in work, or more specifically, the actions they have already taken to resolve the problem before coming to you. You may notice that underneath anger is concern about equity or fairness, or a desire for things to run more smoothly.

What words would you use to comment on their commitment, talent, or investment?

3. Search

What "babies" (constraints, demands, pressures) might be in the "back seat" of the leader's "car"? What constraints or pressures might the administrator be facing? Consider budget shortfalls; lack of time, resources, or staff; interruptions; illness; market pressures; safety constraints; shipping problems; poorly designed processes; lack of information; lack of insight into the pressures of the job; operation limitations; bottlenecks; misunderstandings; or lost data. We will cover the most common root causes of workplace frustrations in Chapter Nine.

At this step, I think of myself as the mythical Sherlock Holmes: dispassionate, analytical, and open to any possibility or surprise. The main goal in this step is to replace negative assumptions and judgments about personalities with curiosity about pressures or constraints of the setting. Assume that the boss is reasonable and invested in doing a good job.

Your assumption that there is a reason for the supervisor's behavior (Third Assumption) rather than he or she is a jerk (First Assumption) can be stated simply. It can be as commonplace as, "The boss isn't usually late. She's under a lot of pressure right now trying to finish up her year-end report and budget. Maybe she forgot. I'll text her."

Brainstorm known or possible constraints and pressures of the other party in the situation you identified. It's amazing how quickly you will be able to think of possibilities once you shift to Third Assumption. Note possible situational reasons for the predicament you are addressing.

4. *Explore*

What actions might your direct report or colleague take to open the dialogue and problem solve? What might be a reasonable first step? A conversation? Arranging a cross-functional meeting? Identify three or four steps.

The alternatives to blame take skill and courage, but they are simple and effective; they are easily within reach, and just like flooding, they can become a default reaction to disagreement and frustration.

How to stop flooding: regret, awareness, choice

If we flood regularly in response to frustration, we will be sorely disappointed if we expect to never lose our tempers again. Like most habits, we can't flip a switch and make flooding go away. It takes time and effort to rewire the brain.

There are three phases to eliminate flooding. The first phase occurs *after* we have flooded. We relive the event in our minds and realize, "Shoot, I flooded." Second is awareness *as it is happening*. This is great progress, because we can shift our thinking to regain control of our emotions. During the third phase, we realize we *could* flood and choose not to. The pause between event and reaction gives us tremendous freedom and confidence to handle life's irritations and disputes.

Unless we are in imminent physical danger, the reason we flood is not because of the event, but because of our thinking. We can drag ourselves back to neutral and ask again, "What could be rational reasons for the other person's behavior?" This assignment shifts brain activity to the cortex. Let's explore these three phases in detail.

1. Regret after the fact

Our first attempts to stop flooding may come too late to avoid a cascade of adrenaline, hormones, cortisol, and the forceful behaviors that result. Initially, insights will occur *after* the body has calmed enough to analyze behavior. This may not happen until several hours after the incident. Flooding is such a physiological hit that the rational, analytical part of the brain doesn't come back online immediately. We should not be discouraged. Even noticing our response and calling it by its medical term, flooding, is progress!

If we make a commitment to stop flooding and then become angry regardless, we should be very careful not to get caught in blame's stinky twin: harsh self-criticism. If we beat ourselves up for "losing control," we will feel hopeless and stop trying. Flooding is a habit. Reprogramming our minds takes many, many repetitions.

There is no finer sensation in life than that which comes with victory over one's self.
—Vash Young

I worked with a construction company on the West Coast that specializes in digging street trenches for utilities. For years the firm tolerated flooding across the company. However, they decided to take a stand on flooding after a passing driver threw trash at one of their crews, and the crew chief, Ricardo, jumped in his truck and chased the driver through city streets.

The company decided on a two-prong approach. They invited me to offer a seminar on the physiology of flooding and preventive strategies, and as a team we created the first draft of a policy on flooding at work.

During the seminar, the employees were thoughtful and reflective and started using the language immediately. A month after my visit I followed up with Ricardo. He told me that although he personally hadn't flooded in the last month, one of his crew flooded at the bank immediately after the seminar!

He said they all laughed about it the next day, and Ricardo reminded the employee that the elimination of flooding is not an overnight undertaking. I love this anecdote, because the crew chief was now coaching his employees. What a great way for Ricardo to embrace the techniques!

Flooding isn't always accompanied with a red face, bulging veins, and outbursts. Women don't flood as quickly and intensely as men. Women tend to have a long, long fuse. However, simmering resentment is just as harmful as the more aggressive forms of flooding. Heart disease is the number-one killer of men *and* women.

Remember: inflammatory venting doesn't help. Drama-venting makes it more likely that we will flood the next time we face a frustration. The solution is to get our arms around our thinking patterns and train our brain to use different pathways. If we make a commitment to stop, and flood regardless, we can use our regret as motivation

2. Awareness of feelings

Identify the earliest cues that you are losing control. How does your body manifest the emotional stress that is the hallmark of flooding? Is it shallow breathing, a tight gut, or tension in your neck and shoulders? Is it pulsing, pounding, tense, anxious, irritable, or frantic? Learn to identify the early physiological signals of flooding so you can short circuit the reflexive response.

Recognize that if you are flooding, it may be best to walk away to tamp down the cascade of emotions. Later in this chapter, we will look at specific techniques to use if you are actively flooding.

3. Realize there is a choice

In the third phase, we can consciously choose how to react. *As the incident is occurring,* we realize we can flood or not. Which choice is the most useful to achieve our goal?

Many individuals believe they cannot stop flooding once they lose their temper. However, when I trained to work with domestic abuse victims, police officers reported that the vast majority of aggressors stop their violence when the police ring their doorbell. In many ways, we do have control over our emotions.

Whom do you target at work?

Common workplace targets can include new hires, senior employees, colleagues, bosses, upper management, unions, temps, human resources, IT, other departments, a sister company, and so on.

If you work in a corporation, you or your colleagues might scapegoat engineering, purchasing, operations, sales, the executive team, the stockholders, your president, the CFO, the board, suppliers, customer services, shipping, operators, technicians, OSHA, quality control, your parent company, or another plant or shift.

Targeted groups in government or social services include politicians, clients, citizens, families, youth, corporations, commissioners, legislators, the mayor, PACs, lobbyists, city council, or the governor.

If you work in a college or university, targets are often deans, commissioners, students, faculty, unions, tenured professors, parents, teaching assistants, K–12 education, disciplines, or departments.

The lists are endless. When do you get energy from self-righteous indignation and contempt? When do you and your colleagues use attacks on others as a form of entertainment and stimulation? Again, if no person or group comes to mind, think about your emotions. What people or groups are on your list of pet peeves? When you flood, who is on the receiving end? Whom do you resent? Who makes you mad?

Be honest; this thinking is almost universal. Write down the groups or people that come to mind. You will use this list in Chapter Eight.

Flooding at home

Sometimes we save our worst behavior for the people we love. Many of my clients report that they manage their anger and irritability quite well at work; however, their behavior at home is an entirely different story.

For many, emotional meltdowns occur at the end of the working day, when we face the second wave of daily demands—the drain of maintaining a home and attending to the needs and idiosyncrasies of partners, pets, children, meals, laundry, bills, and errands at a time when our physical and emotional stamina is depleted.

If we flood with children, we damage ties to family members who are a source of pride and intimacy. Children are masterminds at both passive and aggressive responses to adult flooding. They can act out in ways that demand our attention, including depression, truancy, running away, suicide attempts, panic attacks, eating disorders, sexual promiscuity, and chemical dependency. Children create paybacks for emotional attacks and outbursts from their parents. I've worked with more than one CEO who was struggling with this situation.

Flooding at home has serious consequences on the intellectual and physical development of children. If you cannot consistently be a calm and reliable parent, please seek professional help. Look for resources with your doctor, your employee assistance program, a local mental health clinic, loved ones, or your faith community.

Settings or issues that set us off

Some of us do not target specific individuals or groups. We are more vulnerable to flooding and negativity when we face specific situations. We might have a difficult time when we fly, prepare taxes or pay bills, drive in rush hour, attend a sporting event, wait in line, check the stock market, or watch the news. We may have a particular weakness for flooding when technology fails.

Some individuals are prone to overreacting in areas of their lives where they have the least self-confidence. I have fairly strong confidence in my ability to solve conflict, so it takes quite a bit to knock me off center. However, I am relatively inept with technology, and I become frustrated very quickly over what others might consider a minor snafu.

Jot down the situations or places during which you frequently feel irritation or start to flood. See if there's a relationship between a tendency to flood and feeling insecure about your skills in that area.

Techniques that stop flooding

Many people have contributed to the research on cognitive therapy and negative self-talk. Among the most well-known psychologists are Kenneth Burns and Martin Seligman. Their books helped me develop my early insights into the relationship between thinking, mood, and behavior.

As you start to become conscious of your patterns, you can derail the flooding response by paying attention to how you think. If you feel yourself starting to flood, use any of the following techniques.

In Chapter Two, I shared one of my favorite techniques, "Walnut brain." Here are six more.

1. Ask, "What am I saying to myself? Is it helping me?" We don't have to believe everything we think. When you start feeling tense ask, "Is what I'm saying to myself helping me? Is it strengthening my relationships and helping me reach my goals?" If the answer is no, ask your brain for additional ways to frame the situation.

2. Review the facts. Is there a "baby in the back seat"? Why might this problem exist? We can give ourselves the assignment of generating multiple scenarios of why reasonable people might behave in the manner we are witnessing. As I mentioned earlier, this technique requires that we utilize the cortex.

3. Ask, "Is what I'm saying to myself reasonable and realistic?" It's not necessary to adopt a habit of forced optimism; in some studies, optimism was found to be a less useful coping mechanism than pessimism.

But what about realism? What is reasonable? This question will counter the negativity bias of the brain and our tendency to catastrophize or inflame a stressor. Catastrophizing is defined as the mental rehearsal of everything that can go wrong following a particular event. It is a surefire way to crank up anxiety and dread. Instead, we can ask ourselves, "What's reasonable and realistic?"

4. Finish the following phrase three times. "At least it's not . . ." is the opposite of inflammatory thinking and finishing the phrase multiple times is soothing to the nervous system.

I witnessed an RN use this technique after a driver clipped the rear corner of her car on a freeway. There was considerable damage to her vehicle, and the other driver didn't stop. She was astute enough to know her heart was racing and her blood pressure was soaring. She worked to calm her body by using various versions of "At least it's not . . ." Her dialogue included, "At least I have really good insurance." "At least when the other car bumped me I stayed in my lane." "At least no one was hurt." She was a pro at using this technique to calm her body.

5. Whatever we focus on expands in our minds. During rush-hour traffic, people often tailgate and abruptly change lanes. Many times, when I am in this situation, I start to get tense. Shifting my attention to the people who do not drive that way is an effective antidote. There are lots of people who drive with caution and courtesy. I do not lose track of what the hotheads are doing, but I can lower my stress by not obsessing about their behavior.

6. Say, "I can be effective or self-righteous—pick one." This is one sentence that I found particularly effective when I was breaking my flooding habit. I still use this phrase frequently while on hold, waiting an endless amount of time for someone to pick up my call. I know that if I become irritable and indignant while I wait, when the service technician finally gets to my call, I will not be able to problem solve.

Before you move on, pick one or two of these techniques, and post it where you will see it frequently. Once it becomes a habit, return to this chapter, and add another skill to your anti-flooding arsenal.

Raise the positivity quotient in your life

Let's look at changes we can make to support positive energy in our lives. The more connectedness and success are within reach, the less we'll be vulnerable to anger and denigrating others.

1. Change channels. In a study by HeartMath, just fifteen minutes of listening to grunge rock resulted in increased feelings of hostility, fatigue, sadness, and tension, and led to significant reductions in mental clarity. If you tune in to music, radio, or TV programs that use inflammatory thinking to draw an audience, consider limiting your time or stop completely. Why allow toxic, negative energy into your life? It will strengthen the neurons that fire reactions of contempt. Are you in a better mood, more effective, or more fun to be around after listening to an hour of hate radio? Inflammatory programs tap reflexive responses. Hate DJs are on a mission to increase ratings and revenues, and they are willing to do it at your expense. Inflammatory programing is not interested in your health or well-being, your ability to parent, or your career.

I take responsibility for what circuitry I purposely exercise and stimulate. In an attempt to diminish the power of my fear/anger response, I intentionally chose not to watch scary movies or hang out with people whose anger circuitry is easily set off. I consciously make choices that directly impact my circuitry. Since I like being joyful, I hang out with people who value my joy.
—Jill Bolte Taylor, neuroanatomist

If we listen to inflammatory radio on the way to work, we will already be irritated when we walk into the office: hormones, adrenaline, and blood pressure will be elevated; and we will be less equipped to handle our daily allotment of frustrations.

2. Exercise! While watching television is one of the least effective activities, it is also one of the most frequently used activities for combating a negative mood. Exercise is one of the most effective. Walk with neighbors, get a pet, hike, hunt, camp in the woods, start a yard project, garden, paint, tinker in the garage and create something to donate, bike, or take the kids for a walk around a lake (a favorite Twin Cities activity) and watch the moon rise.

3. Pay attention to what you eat. High sugar consumption impairs cognitive abilities according to a 2012 study by UCLA authors R. Agrawal and F. Gomes-Pinilla. If breakfast consists of a doughnut and supersized Mountain Dew, our bodies don't have the nutrients they need to sustain calming energy. Foods that are saturated with fat and sugar can upset equilibrium and wreak havoc with mood.

4. Avoid harsh self-criticism. We can make a commitment to identify and eliminate self-blame, as it leads to depression, lack of energy, and the desire to blame others as a means of escaping feelings of hopelessness. In Chapter Eight, we'll look at a technique that helps eliminate harsh, negative feelings about ourselves.

In her groundbreaking book *Self-Compassion,* Kristina Neff presents research that shows self-compassion results in more personal growth than harsh self-criticism.

5. Take advantage of the helper's high. We deserve the feelings of bliss that are associated with compassion and offering a helping hand. We can find volunteer work that fits our schedules, interests, and talents. We can go out of our way to befriend someone at work. Remember: even small acts of kindness release endorphins.

Improved mental health was more closely linked to giving than receiving help, according to a study of more than 2,000 individuals by behavioral scientist C. Schwartz and colleagues. Don't stop because you think you have nothing to offer. It takes very little to make a difference in another person's life.

In a study of high-risk youth from impoverished neighborhoods and struggling families, Jennifer Crocker of Ohio State University found that the minority of adolescents who did not end up in the juvenile correction system, who resisted crime and drugs, and who finished high school had one consistent trait in common. They answered the following question in the affirmative: "Do you have someone to talk to about the things that trouble you?" *One link* to a caring individual allowed them to thrive in an environment that overwhelmed their peers. Consider programs similar to Big Brothers Big Sisters, or find individuals in your extended family who would thrive with a bit of extra attention and encouragement.

The more we turn away from self-regard to wipe the tears from the eyes of another, the more—incredibly—we are able to bear, to heal, and to transcend our own suffering. This was their true secret to joy.
—Douglas Abrams, *The Book of Joy* with His Holiness the Dalai Lama and Archbishop Desmond Tutu

---

6. We can surround ourselves with positive people who know how to build and maintain lasting relationships. Every human aches for positive companionship, laughter, and vitality. It's what nature intends. We must do what it takes to replace sources of negative energy with warmth and affection.

We can find positive people who are worthy of our investment at work, in clubs, in faith communities, and in our neighborhood, and we can volunteer at hospitals, food pantries, and youth programs.

People with strong support systems are more likely to avoid disease and maintain higher levels of health. Social support is a natural antidote to tension and stress.

We can find and associate with people who laugh, invest in others, are effective at problem-solving, enjoy long-term intimate relationships, and don't overreact to life's inevitable irritations. These people aren't naïve. As Einstein noted, a harmonious, positive life requires *skill.* "Any intelligent fool can move in the opposite direction."

7. Start rituals of appreciation. We can express our gratitude before meals; make a mental list of all the things for which we are grateful before we fall asleep; and write notes, emails, and letters to loved ones. Martin Seligman found that individuals who wrote and delivered a letter of appreciation had long-lasting increases in happiness—*on the person who sent the note!*

Both abundance and lack exist simultaneously in our lives, as parallel realities. It is always a conscious choice which secret garden we tend.
—Sarah Ban Breathnach

---

8. Develop a meditation practice or join a faith community. Find a community that increases a sense of compassion and positive energy. People who had open-heart surgery were ten times more likely to survive if they had a network of support and spiritual faith.

9. Find mentors. Like the parable at the end of the first chapter, we can find the people in our "village" who sustain and support our growth.

We can spend time with them and watch how they handle tough situations and events. Through observation and conversation, they can teach us about their approaches, philosophy, and skills. They don't have fewer challenges and frustrations than the rest of the world; however, they think about life differently than people who are cynical and hostile, and therefore their lives are dramatically more positive and satisfying.

When my son was a toddler, I often talked to his daycare provider about situations that perplexed me. She taught me very effective techniques for putting him to sleep, avoiding power struggles, and managing temper tantrums. I didn't have these skills beforehand, but I learned I could seek out people who did and learn from them.

10. Use crisis as an opportunity for solidarity. Once we remove blame from our emotional repertoire, problems become opportunities for teams, leaders, and organizations to bond. Situations that once seemed insurmountable become occasions to build new relationships and deepen existing ones.

Without blame, a crisis becomes an occasion to develop new skills and discover previously hidden facets of other people's experiences, training, and capacities. The resulting feelings of achievement and camaraderie reinforce the belief that our colleagues are good people and committed to a worthy cause.

The opportunity and ability to accomplish a task that no one could achieve alone is an ancient, powerful motivator. It is an intrinsic high that makes work meaningful.

Once blame is banished, errors and glitches become opportunities to experience the endorphins associated with the helper's high.

The most natural human response to catastrophe is to pull together.
—Thomas Glass, Johns Hopkins School of Public Health

Despite our fears about human nature, multiple studies of natural disasters reveal that unless a population is already distressed, crime rates actually drop during catastrophes. The British called this innate reaction "the blitz spirit," a self-organized movement of cooperation that developed during the intense and prolonged bombing of England during World War II.

When I visited St. Paul's Cathedral in London, I was touched by the photographs of very young and very old men and women, grandparents, and mothers forming bucket brigades and rescue crews to assist the wounded and save London's most treasured buildings from burning. This ability to create order out of chaos occurred at a time when the municipal government and police departments were barely functioning. This intrinsic instinct to react collectively in groups helps the human race pull together, adapt, and survive.

We can become sensitive to the energy around us and, as much as possible, gravitate toward individuals and groups that support and nurture us.

8

Reciprocity: The Most Reliable Predictor of Behavior

"The heart before you is a mirror. See there your own form."
—Shinto parable

Understanding reciprocity is critical to work and life. It is the intrinsic drive to match others' behaviors, and for others to match ours. Anthropologists find this pattern across the globe.

There are three kinds of reciprocity, but for our purposes, we will focus on two of the three: positive and negative reciprocity. I'll briefly mention the third, which is the reciprocity of indifference.

I feel the reciprocity of indifference when I'm in an environment that is crowded and rushed, such as a New York City shopping district or a college hallway crammed with passing students. There are too many individuals for us to process, and not making eye contact or greeting others is a way for the nervous system to avoid becoming overloaded. Hence we enter a state of indifference, which is reciprocated by the people passing us.

I've also seen this happen in workplace settings when individuals become hesitant to say "Good morning." This is also contagious, and I've seen teams identify and reverse this norm in conflict resolution projects when team members agree that their violation of this common courtesy sets a negative tone.

However, in this chapter we will focus primarily on positive and negative reciprocity because they have the most bearing on conflict and its resolution. Reciprocity is everywhere in our lives, and it is *the most reliable predictor of human behavior.* We are on the receiving end of thousands of acts of behaviors that mirror our actions. The type of reciprocity we create (positive or negative) deeply influences our success, resiliency, and relationships.

When he was in his eighties, my father told me a story that illustrates the steadfastness of reciprocity. During World War II, he had been an American Marine in the Pacific Islands. On Christmas morning, his battalion was ordered to storm a small island off the shore of Australia that was occupied by Japanese troops. The plan was to proceed up the beach to push back the first line of defense, return to shore to regroup, and wait for additional orders.

As they returned to the beach in the midst of chaos and confusion, he heard the disconcerting sound of a woman's voice ringing out, "Hey, Yank! Do you want a cup of coffee?" He turned and saw, incredulously, two civilians from the Australian Salvation Army setting up a stand to distribute coffee at the water's edge. In a gesture of positive reciprocity, they were thanking the Marines for protecting Australia on Christmas morning.

And then, the cycle of reciprocity turned again. Just before the end of the war, my father, who was suffering from malaria, was on leave in California. As he finished his meal at a diner, he noticed two Australian Salvation Army workers eating breakfast and quietly paid for their meals as he left.

Individuals often repay kindness even when they don't feel obligated. In another story about Christmas and coffee, at a Connecticut Starbucks, more than 1,000 customers paid for the coffee of a stranger behind them in an unbroken sequence. They each made a split-second decision: they intrinsically leaned in to repay the kindness.

At the other end of the emotional spectrum, the city of Chicago experienced 3,475 shooting victims in 2017, more than New York City and Los Angeles combined, according to Urban Institute. Staff from UI interviewed 345 of the city's young adults between November 2017 and February 2018. Of those interviewed, one in three said they carried a gun, ranging in frequency from always to rarely.

However, 93 percent said they carried the gun for self-protection, and 84 percent reported they carried a weapon to protect friends/family members (K. Robertson, October 17, 2018).

Anthropologist and MD Gary Slutkin started CeaseFire when he returned to the United States after studying the spread of AIDS in Africa. During his time overseas, gun violence increased dramatically in the United States, and he noticed a parallel between the spread of disease in Africa and the spread of inner-city violence in the United States.

Slutkin viewed gun violence as a spreading virus, and CeaseFire (or in some cities, Cure Violence) trained former gang members to go to the ICU, or even more tragically, the morgue, to plead with family members not to reciprocate acts of violence against them or their families.

Once we understand the reliability of reciprocity, we can put it to work for our benefit. Individuals tell me that understanding reciprocity dramatically changes their behavior. For the first time, they understand why making negative assumptions almost guarantees negative outcomes. They also realize that by changing their view of a difficult situation, they are able to alter the end result.

We can observe reciprocity on both the macro (large-scale) and micro (small-scale) level. On the macro level, we can observe reciprocity between two nations as they match or exceed other country's threats, assaults, diplomats expelled, invasions, or armaments. At the micro level, we witness reciprocity when one individual extends a hand for a handshake and the other person mirrors the behavior.

Reciprocity is so reliable that individuals do *not* match emotional tone only 4 percent of the time, according to John Gottman. Gottman studied reciprocity in his psychology lab at the University of Washington for more than twenty years. By collecting biofeedback data on couples discussing tense issues in their relationships, Gottman was able to predict the outcome of their conversations with 96 percent accuracy by listening to the first three minutes.

According to Gottman, if the initiator opens a conversation with a harsh setup, his or her partner returns the aggression with 96 percent reliability. However, positive reciprocity is just as reliable. When the initiator opens the conversation with appreciation and warmth, the conversation ends on that note 96 percent of the time.

As I mentioned previously, I experienced this matching of negative and positive behaviors seamlessly in the story presented in the Epilogue.

Our behaviors trigger the same in others

Some forms of reciprocity are very subtle. Others are massive and impossible to miss. Individuals "catch" negative behaviors and reciprocate, even after a single incident of low-intensity rudeness, according to a 2018 study by Foulk, Woolum, and Erez at the University of Florida. Recipients of the disrespectful behavior experienced negative emotions, made negative assumptions about others, and reciprocated hostile behaviors. This phenomenon could carry "major consequences for people, for organizations, and perhaps for society as a whole."

We can see negative reciprocity at work in every aspect of our lives, such as:

- Returning an insult to a colleague or stranger.
- Making obscene gestures to an aggressive driver.
- No longer extending dinner invitations to an individual who never returns the overture.
- Sabotaging computer systems after being callously fired.

On the opposite end of the spectrum, positive behaviors are reciprocated by:

- Repaying a kindness from a colleague or stranger.
- Standing up for someone who has defended us.
- Leaving an extravagant tip for an outstanding waiter or waitress.
- Lending a tool to a helpful neighbor.
- Buying lunch for a coworker who has previously picked up the check.

- Remembering the anniversaries or birthdays of someone who faithfully remembers yours.
- Speaking well of a company that laid off employees with genuine regret and respect.

Kindness is also contagious. In a 2016 article in *Scientific American* Jamil Zaki, a psychologist at Stanford, reported individuals not only imitate positive actions but also the spirit underlying them. He wrote, "When we see others around us acting in generous or kind or positive ways, we are more inclined to act that way ourselves."

Cycles of Contempt and Courage

Cycles of Contempt and Courage are circular flowcharts of positive and negative reciprocity. During seminars, participants are given an opportunity to draw both types of cycles. They are powerful tools to visualize how our behavior is seen, interpreted, and returned by the receiver. More than once, participants have been so impressed by their insights that they take their work back to their workplaces (or families) and used them to problem solve.

The quickest way to grasp reciprocity is through examples. We'll look at two cycles drawn by seminar participants. In each case, we'll see a problem that the attendee is experiencing and approach it using First Assumption. We can predict that the interactions will turn into a Cycle of Contempt, damage the relationship, and lower the odds that the problem will be solved. Then we'll tackle the same problem again in a Cycle of Courage using Third Assumption. In the second round, we'll see vastly different outcomes, a strengthened relationship, and progress toward resolution.

Cycles make the mental models we are using a bit more realistic because *for the first time we track how the other party responds to our behavior.* And we'll see that the most impressive part of reciprocity is that the other party's behavior validates our original negative assumption.

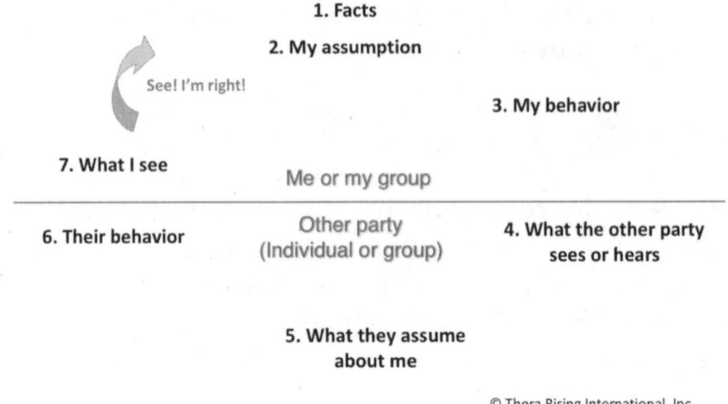

Figure 8.1. The reciprocity template.

When we draw cycles, the person who is drawing the cycle is on top of the horizontal line and the other party (person or group) is below the line.

1. Identify the facts about a situation we would like to improve. We try not to add interpretations or speculate about motives in step one. We just jot down the facts.
2. If we are drawing a negative cycle (a Cycle of Contempt), after Step 2, we blame the problem on the people in the bottom half of the cycle.
3. We record our behavior based on our thinking. In negative cycles, behavior is typically some form of attack and/or avoid.
4. We go below the horizontal line and put ourselves in the shoes of the other party. How does our behavior look to them? What do they see or hear?
5. What assumptions does the other person make about us and our motives? Imagine what the other person might think about us given how we are treating them. This step is a good exercise in empathy.
6. How does the other party behave based on their assumption of us? In Cycles of Contempt, the recipient's behavior is often as negative, or more so, than ours.

7. Back above the line now, to our world. What do we observe? The most insidious aspect of reciprocity is that the other party's negative behavior confirms our negative assumption. "See, I was right!"

Let's move to two examples from our seminars, and these reliable cycles will become crystal clear.

Cycle of Contempt: Project managers and architects

Lenore was a construction project manager (PM) at a design and build company in Montana. For ten years there had been ongoing tension between the project managers who oversaw site construction and the architects who created the blueprints from which the PMs and their crews worked. The PMs were held accountable for overruns, and fiscal conservatism was one of their company's selling points and a source of pride.

Lenore thought the architects lived in a fantasy world, oblivious to the day-to-day realities of material and budget constraints. She and other PMs felt the architects wasted time and money designing features that were impressive, but frivolous and unnecessary.

Figure 8.2. Cycle of Contempt: Project managers and architects.

Lenore drew a Cycle of Contempt (Figure 8.2) to address the ongoing tension. She started her cycle with the facts:

1. **Facts:** "The architect's designs are over budget."
2. **Our assumption:** Since Lenore was drawing a Cycle of Contempt, she used First Assumption to guide her thinking about why the architect's designs were consistently out of alignment with the client's budget. It wasn't difficult for her to write the next statement; it was an opinion that was frequently expressed among the project managers: "Architects have big egos and live in fantasy land!"
3. **Our behavior:** She wrote down the unspoken norm among the project managers: "Hide pools of money. If we have 20 million for a building, we tell the architects we have 15 million." When Lenore went underneath the horizontal line, she crossed into the world of the architects and had to put herself in their shoes.
4. **What the architects see:** Lenore had to guess how the architects viewed her behavior. After pondering this situation from the architect's perspective she wrote, "Money always pops up at the last minute." Perhaps a newly hired architect would not question discrepancies in the budget figures during their first project, but by the third or fourth building, they would realize that the PMs were not being honest.
5. **The architect's assumption:** Lenore looked at her cycle for a few moments. Again, she put herself in the shoes of the architects and thought, "If I were an architect and I knew that the PMs were consistently misrepresenting budget parameters, how would I view them?" She wrote, "The PMs are liars, and you can't trust them."
6. **The architect's behavior:** She asked herself, "What would the architects do to retaliate for the dishonesty of the project managers?"

"Ignore our warnings," she wrote. She started laughing; for the first time she realized how the two groups had created a ludicrous, self-fulfilling power struggle. When Lenore moved back above the horizontal line in her Cycle of Contempt, she returned to the world of project managers.

7. **What we see:** She wrote, "Every year this problem gets worse!" When the architects dismissed the budget concerns of the project managers, they came full circle, validating the PMs negative assumptions. "See! We're right!"

The validation of the original assumption is the most fascinating, heartbreaking, and valuable part of the Cycle of Contempt. When the PMs saw the architects ignoring their budget advice, it validated their beliefs that the architects were not team players. The PMs concluded that the architects were aloof and uninterested in the fiscal aspects of their work. Their worst fears were confirmed, and they felt justified in continuing to denigrate the architects. It became obvious that the PMs' thinking was part of the perpetual tension and mistrust between the groups.

Cycles validate the negative opinions of both groups. Unless someone steps out of the repetitive cycle, the architects will continue to view the PMs as tiresome, dishonest, and averse to experimenting with new features and designs.

Cycle of Courage: Project managers and architects

To break a Cycle of Contempt, we start by changing step two, the assumption. Often the ability to identify the other party's constraints and pressures requires a conversation. I learned that the PMs' bonuses were based on finishing their projects "on time and under budget." But the architects didn't receive a year-end bonus. What was shaping their behavior? Lenore and I opened the dialogue, and as you will see, what we discovered shifted their relationships; she had an opportunity to create positive reciprocity with the architects. Lenore realized she had the power to end the standoff between the two groups.

In Cycles of Courage, participants use Third Assumption. What if the perpetual tension over the budget *wasn't* caused by the annoying personalities of the architects? What else could it be? Again, this is similar to giving your brain a new command: Why would a reasonable person behave in this manner? Are there system problems between the two groups? Are they working off different sets of data? Are their bonuses or performance measures based on criteria that pit the project managers and architects against each other?

When Lenore considered situational possibilities, she realized she was facing many barriers to cooperation including a process problem (the steps and sequence used to accomplish a task). The architects were not too egotistical or temperamental to worry about cost. The real cause of tension was the architects worked in isolation to create the blueprints and then delivered their designs to the PMs for pricing. The two groups waited too long into the design phase to start shaping each other's work, resulting in endless rework. The architects and project managers needed to collaborate and integrate each other's expertise earlier in the process. To resolve the tension they needed to change the sequencing of their work.

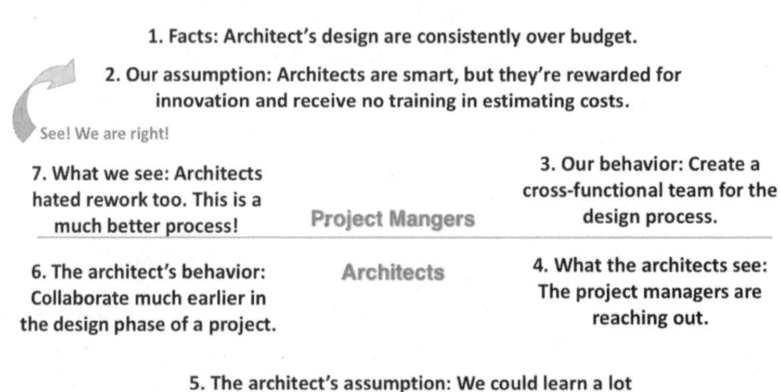
1. Facts: Architect's design are consistently over budget.
2. Our assumption: Architects are smart, but they're rewarded for innovation and receive no training in estimating costs.
See! We are right!
7. What we see: Architects hated rework too. This is a much better process!
Project Mangers
3. Our behavior: Create a cross-functional team for the design process.
6. The architect's behavior: Collaborate much earlier in the design phase of a project.
Architects
4. What the architects see: The project managers are reaching out.
5. The architect's assumption: We could learn a lot about pricing and eliminate endless re-work.
© Thera Rising International, Inc.

Figure 8.3. Cycle of Courage: project managers and architects.

In Cycles of Courage, when participants return to their problem, they do not change the facts; they change how they think about the source of the problem. Lenore wrote again:

1. **Facts:** "The architect's designs are consistently over budget."
2. **Assumptions:** In this round, Lenore's thinking was less personality-based and less inflammatory. She considered two possible problems: "Architects are rewarded for being innovative, and receive no training in estimating costs." As her thinking changed, Lenore's behavior changed.
3. **Behavior:** "Create a cross-functional team to start pricing earlier in the design process." How would the architects view the shift? Lenore went underneath the horizontal line and put herself in the architects' shoes and responded from the architect's perspective.
4. **What the architects see:** "The project managers are reaching out."
5. **The architect's assumption:** "We could learn a lot from them and eliminate endless rework."
6. **The architect's behavior:** "Collaborate much earlier in the design phase of the project." When Lenore went above the horizontal line, she resumed her role as a project manager.
7. **What the project managers see:** "Architects hated rework too. This is a much better process." And again, she confirmed her assumption. "See! We are right!"

Lenore realized that if the two groups created more opportunities for dialogue and discussion during the design phase, the architects would become more knowledgeable about costs, and project managers would learn more about the pressures that drive the architects.

When the two groups discussed the tension between their departments, the project managers were surprised to learn how much business savvy the architects actually had—but from a totally different perspective.

The architects were striving for a goal that they had never articulated with the construction division. One of the biggest motivators for the architects was having their work featured in an architectural journal. The architects knew that the most prized criteria for this honor was innovation! The architects who excelled at paradigm-shifting designs were rewarded with high-status projects. Within their industry, originality was one of their principal ways of contributing to the prestige and reputation of the company, and attracting affluent clients.

Once the project managers understood the architects' motives, their irritability and judgment of the architects shifted, and the new mindset was clearly communicated to the architects.

The supervisors and new hires' Cycle of Contempt

I was invited to work with a company that had extraordinarily difficult working conditions. The men who worked on these crews repaired never-ending miles of railroad tracks and performed taxing manual labor in the best and worst of Minnesota's extreme weather. The crews traveled continuously, moving along the track and changing hotel rooms every other night. When they had a day off, they spent it alone, without access to a vehicle, in a barren motel room watching TV.

Every three months, they went home for two weeks. Their hourly pay was so low that only substantial amounts of overtime provided a living wage. Their turnover rates were sky-high, and Richard, the human resource manager, wanted to find out exactly why workers were leaving.

During exit interviews, Richard learned that employees did not quit because of time away from home, low hourly pay, or physical hardship. The most frequently cited reason for leaving was being treated with disrespect by the crew chiefs. Richard heard about Thera Rising's work and asked me to collaborate with the supervisors to improve their ability to manage teams in harsh, isolated settings.

During a skill-building seminar, we were working on cycles, and one of the supervisors focused on a frustration that every one of the bosses faced: a newly hired employee whose performance was below standards.

Addressing the problem of an underperforming employee, the crew chief wrote:

1. **Facts:** "A new operator is not pulling his weight."
2. **My assumption:** "The new hire is lazy."
3. **My behavior:** "Embarrass him in front of the other men. Point out his mistakes and make an example out of him."

But when he moved underneath the horizontal line, he put himself in the shoes of the new hire and looked at his own behavior through his employee's eyes.

4. **What the new hire sees:** "My boss sets me up and ridicules me to get a laugh."
5. **The negative conclusion the new hire makes about me:** My boss is a jerk. In fact, the whole company sucks.
6. **The new hire's behavior:** "Find other guys who hate the boss and make his life living hell."
7. **What I see:** "The new hire is a loser and troublemaker."

The supervisor's cycle is as obvious as negative reciprocity gets, and this reality wasn't lost on the crew chief who was drawing it.

During the seminar, all the supervisors hung their Cycles of Contempt on the wall for their peers to read. After the crew chief finished his cycle, the entire class gathered in front of his work in dead silence. No one challenged what he had drawn. They realized as a group that their colleague was dead-on accurate.

For the first time, the chiefs realized how critical their attitudes were in setting the tone for their men. It was contempt that was destroying camaraderie, increasing turnover, and making their jobs more difficult. Once again individuals were confronted with the *self-defeating* nature of their behavior.

The supervisors and new hires' Cycle of Courage

When we analyzed the problem of new hires using Third Assumption, we realized that the root cause was a company policy. The applicants who responded to the company's recruitment efforts had much less skill and experience than entry-level workers in the past.

Fifteen years ago, most of their new hires were graduates of technical schools. They could read schematics and understood the fundamentals of electricity and welding. However, not only were most of their current employees not graduates of a technical school, but the majority were also high school dropouts.

During our discussions, the supervisors acknowledged the declining levels of competency in their hiring pool. However, the company had been running the same on-boarding program for more than fifteen years. The problem wasn't the personalities or motivation of the new hires. In reality, most of their applicants needed more extensive and basic training than their current course provided.

After the supervisor drew his Cycle of Courage, his attitude toward the operators shifted. Richard, the human resource manager, immediately began working with their internal instructors to start assessing the skill level of new hires and redesign their training program. From that point onward, when a new hire floundered, the chiefs were more receptive to problem-solving, coaching, mentoring, and providing on-the-job training.

Using warmth and encouragement rather than contempt, they were more successful in retaining the employees who had the capacity to learn the skills the job required, and the seasoned veterans were relieved when the hostility and negativity of their work situation lifted. For the first time, crews and supervisors had an opportunity to become real teams.

You are the center of your universe

After they work with these cycles, many clients tell me they ask themselves, "How will my actions be perceived?" on a regular basis. You may be surprised how often you change your behavior in reaction to the answer. *Being able to jump ahead and anticipate the sequence of events that follow our assumptions allows us to consciously shape our reactions.*

Before you move on, I recommend you turn back to the reciprocity template (Figure 8.1) and fill out the template twice. Pick a situation that has stymied you. In the first round, Cycle of Contempt, blame the party on the bottom half for the problem. As you complete the cycle, you will see how your behavior looks to them and the reciprocity it triggers.

Then do it again, and write inside your first cycle. Leave number one the same. But change your thinking. Why might this problem exist? Could it be mutual lack of skill or insight? Lack of communication? Different versions of the facts? Hidden pressures or constraints?

In the next chapter, we'll look at the most common causes of workplace tension, and you will learn other possible triggers of conflict to consider. From here on, you can observe these self-fulfilling patterns and use them to your benefit.

9

Five Root Causes of Workplace Conflict and Tension

"The line between good and evil lies in the center of every human heart."
—Alexander Solzhenitsyn

Before we dive into root causes, let's talk about exceptions. In my experience, 97 percent of escalated conflicts were *not* driven by personalities and people. In 3 percent of situations, we discovered that an employee did not have the capacity to do his or her job, and in those instances, we shift to the company's performance development system.

Once in a great while, mental health issues such as depression trigger conflict, and managers need to tap mental health centers or employee assistance programs. Sometimes, working with external resources organizations facilitate interventions for chemical use or drug dependency.

As we will see in Rick's story, on occasion the conflict is so debilitating that it is difficult to assess the competencies of an employee. During power struggles, an individual's "evil twin" emerges, and it can be impossible to discern an employee's potential separate from the stress and fear that is generated by escalated conflict.

If management is unclear about an employee's capacities during heightened conflict, it is prudent to: eliminate any system or policy problems that are interfering with productivity, lower fear, and end any power struggles. Then wait a reasonable period of time for the work environment to stabilize before assessing performance. If under improved conditions an employee cannot meet realistic performance measures, it's time to shift from a conflict resolution process to a performance management system.

There are rare cases in which clients are hiding illegal or unethical behaviors. When we suspect these possibilities are at the root of tension, we need to step out of the conflict resolution process and initiative an investigation.

The five root causes

With awareness of the exceptions, let's look at the reasons conflict escalates in the workplace. *The good news is that the five root causes can be corrected.* However, 100 percent of my clients were not able to fix the root cause because they were caught up in First Assumption and its fallout.

I began to see the reliability of these causes only because I had worked on hundreds of escalated conflicts. There are other recurring causes of tension, but in my experience these are the ones that repeatedly trip up employees and leaders.

I appreciate this list because it is simultaneously broad and concise: 1) a baby in the back seat—a constraint or pressure hidden from view; 2) poorly designed processes; 3) performance measures that pit employees against each other; 4) a mutual lack of skill, insight, or courage; and 5) negative reciprocity.

As you'll see, sometimes organizations unconsciously build barriers into the work, and it behooves us to take the focus off the people and put our attention where it can make a difference.

Before we dive into details, *think about a situation you'd like to improve.* You can use targets you identified in Chapter Seven. As we proceed, you can ask if the root cause we are discussing is the source of the problem you identified.

1. Is there a baby in the back seat?

I always assume that the other party has numerous hidden constraints or pressures shaping his or her behavior. In Chapter Five there were several workplace examples of hidden constraints. Recall the missing supervisor (sick from his hepatitis B medication but dragging himself to work because the boss was short-handed) and the brooding CEO (whose undisclosed vision to rebuild the factory was shattered when the workers went on strike). I've witnessed hundreds of similar stories.

When we make the assumption that hidden pressures are shaping behavior, it takes so little energy to sit down and ask individuals about barriers to productivity. I haven't always immediately discovered a hidden reason. Sometimes it takes time to build trust, or the fear of punishment or organizational retribution is too high. I don't always get the answer I expect or want. But I never regret making the attempt to open the dialogue because I always learn *something*.

In the next chapter, we'll discuss a proven but simple template for initiating these conversations in the spirit of humility and curiosity—a win-win.

However, before we move on to the next root cause, consider what personal or workplace "babies" might be hidden from view in the situation you are trying to improve.

Sometimes just by asking this question, the entire problem shifts. A police officer was drawing his Cycle of Contempt in class, and the situation he was tackling involved his sister-in-law who repeatedly asked him for loans. In the first round, he blamed her and said she was irresponsible and selfish. Annoying! He refused her requests.

In his Cycle of Courage, he wrote down her baby in the back seat. "She asks for money because her husband (my brother) is in prison for a felony, and she's trying to fill the void by purchasing things for her young son." As he allowed himself to take in the reality of her situation, his behavior shifted and he wrote, "Help my sister-in-law create a budget and spend time with my nephew."

What hidden constraints might shape the behavior of the party (person or group) with whom you are frustrated?

2. Poorly designed systems and processes

Poor or nonexistent process design is often a hidden cause of prolonged conflict. We behave differently depending on constraints, demands, peer pressure, anxiety levels, urgency, and so on. This notion is fairly well accepted in academic circles but is not widely recognized in the workplace. Most individuals think about others as static and one dimensional, such as good, selfish, crude, lazy, undependable, trustworthy, or ambitious. In reality, personality is not fixed. Each of us have a range of behaviors from which we choose. Even people who are deemed unsalvageable by the courts have the capacity to behave differently. For example, felons with no hope for parole volunteer to raise seeing-eye dogs and provide hospice care to aging inmates.

The other side of human nature is also true. "Ordinary" people are capable of malfeasance when trapped in corrupt systems. For example, individuals who value integrity and honesty will behave badly when their economic security is at risk. In the book *The Cheating Culture,* author David Callahan documents the decline of formerly trustworthy Sears auto mechanics in the 1990s.

The leadership at Sears headquarters unexpectedly decided to lower the base pay of both managers and mechanics, and announced that both groups could compensate for their drop in income by earning a percentage of every part they sold. Workers and managers alike found themselves in the uncomfortable position of choosing between integrity and economic security.

Within a few years, Sears's sterling customer service ratings plummeted, and eighteen class-action suits and scores of investigations for fraudulent practices were brought against the company. The company was fined $2,000,000,000 for fraud.

Processes and compensation are just two of the dynamics that shape behavior. Workplaces are constantly required to challenge, motivate, and mediate human behavior. At one level this insight means that by changing structure, rewards, and performance criteria, organizations can change behavior. Or when you look through the other side of the lens, if leadership isn't satisfied with current behavior, they can change the conditions that cause undesired outcomes.

Structure has a profound impact on behavior. In the workplace, competitive systems with harsh economic norms result in aggressive, and sometimes unethical, behavior. In contrast, systems that are seen as accessible, fair, rewarding, and cooperative bring out the best in people.

Elliot Aronson conducted experiments loaded with insight for workplaces. Aronson, a specialist in school shootings, analyzed dozens of student shooting perpetrators and eventually turned his attention away from "personality, attitudes, or demographics" to the environment in which this act occurs. His conclusions are chilling. "The root cause of the shootings is the poisonous social atmosphere that exists in almost every public school in this country—atmospheres permeated by daily incidents of exclusion, taunting, bullying, and humiliation."

Of particular value to our purpose is Aronson's ability to improve relationships between elementary students by simply changing the structure in which they learn. Aronson coached teachers to shift from a competitive to a cooperative learning environment, known as the "jigsaw classroom," where student's work was interdependent rather than competitive. Within two weeks, students had gone from taunting to encouraging each other. Lasting friendships were formed across cultural and language differences—differences that had been the basis of exclusion and taunting just days prior to the change.

Alfie Kohn's classic book (and recipient of the American Psychological Association National Psychology Award for Excellence in Media) *No Contest: The Case Against Competition* is a meta-analysis of the impact of competition on self-esteem, relationships, and productivity. Citing hundreds of studies, he concludes that in all three areas cooperation produces superior outcomes. I often see examples of his findings in workplaces.

Poorly designed systems trigger conflict

I had the good fortune of working for a process improvement company early in my career. Learning about system thinking and process mapping made me more effective in every aspect of my work.

First I began to see how much systems and processes drive the day-to-day activities of our world. If we take a quick glance at the ubiquity of systems in our society, it's quite sobering. Our lives are shaped by systems of transportation, weather, education, military, political, ecology, medical, family, agriculture, finance, and so on. Systems are everywhere, and it's useful to see them and understand a bit about how they work.

The key features of systems are interdependency, delicacy, and constant change. Systems are interdependent so change affects everything up and downstream. For a quick example of interdependency we can think about ecosystems and how changes in air temperature affect the westerly winds, which affect the movement of rain, which results in droughts or flooding, the salination of water, the contamination of aquifers, and compromised sea levels.

In the workplace, the hierarchical view places everyone in silos with direction coming from the top, with the expectation that the environment is relatively static.

In a system view, we can visualize handing off our work to other departments and internal customers. It is a more interdependent and collaborative view. A simplified systems perspective of manufacturing might begin with determining trends; completing feasibility studies, building prototypes, and gaining approval of final designs; procuring the necessary raw materials; transforming raw materials into outputs (finished products); transporting to dealers; overseeing leases and sales; tracking warranty, safety, and service data; and studying after-sales information to feed back into the system. Then the whole cycle starts anew as the organization gears up for the next generation of production.

Uncover hot spots by looking at your processes

There are many books and courses on system thinking and process improvement. These techniques are taught at universities, nonprofits, and consulting firms. The information falls under different names and formats, such as Total Quality, the Baldridge Award, Lean, and Process Improvement. You can tap a global network of members, books, and training at *www.ASQ.org*. Dan Madison's book *Process Mapping, Process Improvement and Process Management* is a worthy introductory text.

Processes are the steps of a system. Examples of common processes are hiring, training, payroll, performance management, and so on. For instance, the first step in the hiring process might include determining the need for a new position, defining the job and qualifications, and setting a salary range. The second step might be advertising the position or selecting an employment agency. Next steps might include reviewing applications, and conducting interviews. Each of these acts is a step in the hiring process.

I became interested in process mapping when I realized how quickly and effectively process maps help individuals communicate the complexity of their work and pinpoint bottlenecks, rework, and waste. As you will see in the following story, it is common for process problems to be blamed on one or more employees who become the organization's scapegoat.

How well do most systems and processes work? It depends. How savvy are the leaders about system thinking? When problems occur, do individuals from other departments join together to solve them, or do they break into Cycles of Contempt? Do employees understand the delicate interdependency of their work and take other parts of the process into consideration when they make decisions? Does a university collect feedback from students and roll it into future course offerings and new faculty hiring?

Most workplace systems have a staggering number of processes. Some experts put the number at 2,000! In many organizations, the *majority* of their processes are poorly designed and inefficient. Most workplace processes were never consciously designed; they just evolved.

Imagine the improvements in efficiency and morale if organizations could improve key processes by even 5 percent! W. Edwards Deming, a statistician sent to Japan by the American government after World Word II, taught the Toyota and Honda families about system thinking and statistical variation at a time when Japan had no manufacturing capacity. His success in Japan created demand for his strategies in the United States. Some of his first clients in the United States were General Motors and Ford. Deming believed that 85 to 93 percent of workplace waste originates in systems, not people.

Employees work in a system. It's the job of management to work on the system and improve it, continuously, with their help.
—Myron Tribus

How do we uncover process problems? By engaging in one of the oldest human behaviors: talking to each other.

When I am doing team-building or conflict resolution, I often create a simple process map with clients. Working in small groups and hanging our work on the wall, we use oversized sticky notes for each step. Sticky notes are excellent for the first draft of a process map because they can be lifted and repositioned as many times as necessary. We create the process as it now exists and then look for areas that could be improved.

Even with the most basic process map, individuals can see how much of their conflict relates to dysfunctional processes, not people. The following story illustrates how millions of dollars can be saved once the key players shifted from blame to fixing a catastrophic process problem.

The outlier that dissed the president

Rick narrowly escaped termination after he "lipped off" to the company president. Most of the executive team viewed Rick as an unprofessional, undisciplined hothead who exploited the fact that he was central to one of their most important processes: the production of customized machines, which were the bread and butter of this company.

Rick's job was critical. If a salesperson wanted a custom machine, Rick was the person to see. However, Rick's turnaround on an estimate for customization was *three months!* The sales people were livid; they told me they were losing 25 percent of their orders and millions of dollars due to this delay.

The relationship between Rick and the sales group had deteriorated so badly that during the annual sales meeting, Virg, the vice president, announced, "Rick is our number-one barrier to sales."

The company president told me that Rick would have been terminated months ago if anyone else in the company could have done his job. The president gave me carte blanche to do whatever it would take to "fix him."

By the time I was done collecting background information, I half expected Rick to be a surly, arrogant sociopath. Instead, I found someone who cared so much about his work that we talked for four hours about his frustrations, resentments, attempts to resolve his huge backlog, efforts to speed up the process, his failure to obtain more resources, how he had fought and lost the battle to keep his assistant during a downturn, and how he lacked access to the internal expertise he needed to do his job.

Rick told me that after he heard about Virg's comment at the sales meeting, he lost all his motivation to overcome the backlog, quit working overtime, and fell further behind. It was a textbook example of negative reciprocity.

As Rick's story wound down, I made it very clear that we were about to turn in his resignation as the company scapegoat and take unprecedented steps to fix the problem at its source. I think Rick was shocked at my reaction. He had expected a pep talk about working harder.

During our first conversation, I consciously used the power of connectedness to bond. It's the fastest way to gain commitment to a hard-headed search for solutions. When Rick wrapped up his story, he knew I had truly listened and acknowledged the validity of his frustrations, respected his dedication, and was impressed by the creative ways he tried to resolve the backlog.

Not until this point could I give him the critical feedback he needed to hear. With copious amounts of warmth and humor, I told him the organization could take the lion's share of responsibility for the bottleneck, however, his defensiveness and "complete lack of social skills" with the president did not help.

The relationship we forged during our first meeting allowed me to speak to Rick bluntly. Even though I had only known him for a few hours, Rick laughed good-naturedly at my frank remarks. He knew he had to alter his approach to achieve the change he so desperately needed.

Rick lacked the skill and positional power to address the real problem. The customization quote process that needed improvement spanned three divisions and required the involvement of management four levels above him.

Within a few days of our first meeting, Rick and I sat down with the vice presidents of engineering, operations, and sales. I asked Rick to share his perceptions of the root causes of the current backlog, and as a group, using the sticky notes and flip-chart paper method, we flow-charted the current process for procuring an estimate on customized machines.

In order to create a cost and time estimate, Rick needed the expertise of engineering, sales, software, and operations. However, Rick had no leverage with these internal experts, and no one got credit for helping him.

Rick explained that when he approached a colleague for his or her input on yet another quote, he or she ducked into offices to avoid him. As a result, every piece of information Rick needed to complete his quotes required multiple unreturned emails, phone calls, and walks through the building to strong arm his coworkers for information.

During our meeting, Virg learned that the salespeople (with his encouragement) were loading their requests for estimates with every conceivable feature, knowing full well the customer would never pay the premium dollars it took to include them.

However, customizations were the company's market niche, and complex orders were one of the ways the sales group played up the organization's capacities. Unfortunately, each one of these features added layers of complexity and delays to Rick's work. When Rick attempted to tell the salespeople that the extraneous features made the problem worse, they dismissed him as a slacker, especially after their vice president had personally christened him "the number-one barrier to sales."

Virg dropped his eyes when he realized that someone had told Rick about his denigrating remark. Then Virg spontaneously—and with genuine remorse—apologized for the callous remark. A flash of relief crossed Rick's face.

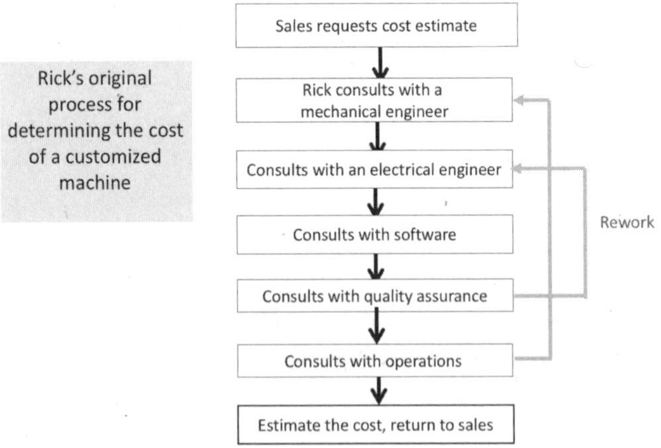

Figure 9.1. Rick's original process, full of rework and delays.

The five of us turned our attention to the wasteful and haphazard process. Rick explained that in the current process, his efforts were linear. In other words, he'd start with mechanical engineering, get their advice, then go to the next group, and so on. However, more often than not the second, third, or fourth person in the process would explain why this version of a customized machine wasn't feasible. For instance, quality assurance might kibosh the dimensions the engineers had recommended because of the manufacturing equipment's limitations. Rick would have to make adjustments to the estimate and start over with the first group. As Rick explained the chaotic nature of the process, the VPs went from resentment to admiration for Rick's efforts.

Virg stepped up first and announced he was changing the process of submitting an order in sales. From here forward, all requests for customized machines had to pass through a gatekeeper who would eliminate extraneous features before they reached Rick's desk. If there were too many superfluous features, the request for a sales estimate was returned to the salesperson. The next change was the creation of a cross-functional team, with representatives from every department giving input, at the same time, on each order.

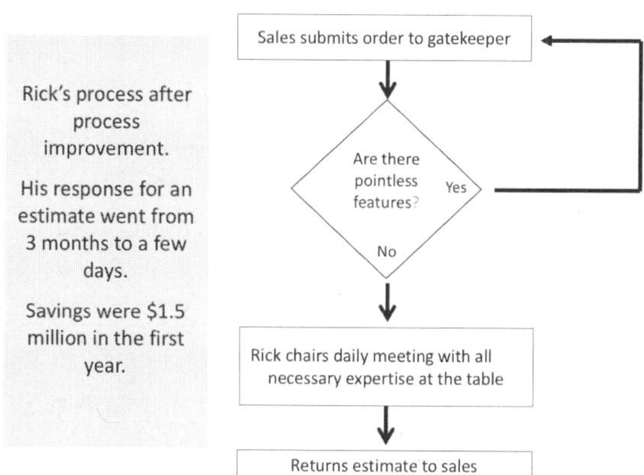

Figure 9.2. Rick's streamlined process saved $1.5 million in the first year.

The next morning, the VPs met with their teams and announced the modifications. Rick began chairing a daily meeting with all the expertise he needed seated at the table. With everyone in the room to review requests and rough out estimates, Rick's process to estimate a customized machine went from three months to a few days.

The sales team was ecstatic. This gave them a tremendous competitive advantage. After the changes were implemented, the president estimated they captured an additional *$1.5 million in sales* the first year!

Once the root cause was identified, everyone in the organization fell over themselves trying to make amends for their previously harsh treatment of Rick. A few months later, Rick, the former recipient of the organization's contempt, was the honored guest at the company's annual sales meeting. He took the podium to talk about the next generation of customized designs.

If system thinking and process mapping are new to you, then tap resources and start to understand this critical aspect of your work. You can start by listing some of your main processes in your work. Which ones are problematic? Could you pull together a group and start problem-solving?

Regardless, if you're at the introductory or mastery level you can ask yourself, "Is a process problem increasing tension between me and the person with whom I'm frustrated?"

3. Performance measures that conflict

Most performance measures, such as quality, speed, and growth, make sense within a department but can cause tension *between* departments. I witnessed this in a hospital setting where the employees in the nursing division were evaluated on multiple measures, including customer satisfaction, and employees in finance were appraised on how quickly patients were discharged. If these systemic conflicts are not verbalized, they can trigger factions and mistrust. If inherent tensions between groups cannot be changed, at least they can be acknowledged, so employees are not as likely to resent the behavior of their colleagues.

The story of the architects and project managers from the previous chapter is a textbook example of how seemingly reasonable performance measures can cause tension between groups. The architects were rewarded for being innovative and attracting the attention of the press. However, innovations take financial resources. Their immediate colleagues in construction received bonuses for finishing projects on time and under budget. They lacked an understanding of these differences and resorted to avoidance and name-calling.

More than once I found that the root cause of conflict between executives and their departments was rooted in the calculations upon which their bonuses were paid. Executives worked specific criteria to maximize his or her bonus, but at the expense of cross-functional collaboration.

I worked with an executive team who decided that a significant barrier to collaboration was bonuses based on departmental goals. They agreed that the executive team's bonus should be set with the same measure—year-end profitability. Twenty-four hours after we agreed on this change, the VP of sales offered the VP of operations (his previous scapegoat) his unfilled employee position to help alleviate the staff shortage in operations. Why did the formerly self-oriented executive suddenly become so cooperative? Because we made it in his best interest to help his colleagues succeed.

When bonuses, systems, award programs, and performance measures are based on departmental goals, silo thinking dominates, despite hand-wringing and platitudes from upper management. When financial rewards are based on cooperation and interdependence, collaborative behavior is acknowledged and rewarded.

Return to the situation you would like to improve, and ask yourself, "Is there tension between me and the person with whom I'm frustrated because our performance measures aren't in alignment?"

4. Mutual lack of skill, insight, or courage

Of the five root causes, this is the one I witness most frequently. Whenever someone acts in a destructive or callous manner, I ask myself, "Is this person lacking skill, insight, or courage?" These questions can save many hours of useless fuming and negativity.

Personally, when I am the one who misses the mark, I analyze my behavior using the same set of questions. These six words—lack of skill, insight, or self-confidence—are a useful way to hold ourselves accountable without sliding into shame, which is debilitating.

The difference between lack of skill, insight, and courage, and the sense of dread that accompanies inflammatory thinking ("This is all *your* fault, you are *totally* worthless, and you will *never* change") is that everyone can become more skillful, more insightful, and more courageous. Lack of skill, insight, and courage is not a fatal condition—it is an invitation to *grow*.

"All the managers are immature!"

The following story conveys a time I was caught off guard by the destructive behavior of a client, flooded, backed up, and approached the problem more effectively. Following a public seminar, the HR director from a large nonprofit agency approached me. Roxanne loved the class and asked me to come to her organization and conduct sessions for their managers. She said their organization was full of negativity and blame, and could definitely benefit from the insights and skills of the class.

On the first day at her organization, I was pleasantly surprised to see Roxanne sitting in the audience, ready to participate for the second time. "Wow, she must be a big fan of the material," I thought naïvely. "It must have made a big impact!"

In the few minutes before the presentation began, people were chatting and enjoying coffee and pastries. A small group of managers sitting together near the front of the room started to discuss an organizational disaster that had occurred the previous year. Due to a new software program, paychecks for the organization had been delayed for more than two weeks. I learned later that the error, which occurred right before Christmas, caused significant problems for most of their employees, and it originated in Roxanne's office.

Roxanne, who was sitting in the back of the room, overheard their private conversation. From across the room, she said loudly, "Are you still talking about that? Do you know why this organization is so screwed up? Because all the managers are immature!"

The room became dead quiet. I was in an uncomfortable spot. My contract with the organization was to facilitate a seminar. I wasn't prepared to resolve this conflict; it was the wrong audience, and it's not what they had asked me to do. I did my best to smooth over her statement and alleviate the negative impact of her remarks, but when I left at the end of the day, I knew the group had not fully recovered from the sting of her insult.

Once I was on my way home, I found myself rerunning the "tape" of Roxanne's words. I thought, "What a jerk!" In an effort to justify my feelings of self-righteousness and anger, I went on a classic "search for stupidity."

It wasn't difficult to find facts to support my negative thinking. Despite the fact that Roxanne seemed to value my message, she started the day by attacking everyone in the room—the very behaviors she had asked me to alleviate!

Suddenly I remembered I had to do two more seminars at her agency. Maybe she would be on vacation; I wanted to avoid her.

Then the arrow of blame turned inward. Maybe *I* was the problem! I hadn't exactly saved the day. Maybe I was a fraud! If I had been Nelson Mandela, the situation would have been a piece of cake. Why hadn't I fixed it? I was really on a roll. I felt angry and powerless, and I was starting to feel my stomach churn. I wondered if I was getting the flu.

I was making myself upset by my *thinking!* Fortunately, I knew I could alleviate my distress simply by changing what I was saying to myself.

Before I understood these principles, the thinking patterns of blame, self-criticism, and their accompanying physical reactions were daily experiences for me. However, for three years I had practiced the baby in the back seat technique and alternatives to blame. Now it was relatively easy to become aware of the change in my body chemistry and identify the cause.

I started laughing because I realized I blamed Roxanne because she had blamed the supervisors because the supervisors had blamed her department. I started my analysis over.

A more useful way to think about human imperfections

Let's return to Roxanne and look at her behavior first. Then I will look at my own. Might her actions reflect a lack of skill? Could she have accomplished her goal by talking to the group privately and saying something similar to, "Are you talking about the mistake we made last year in payroll? I know it caused hardship, but when managers keep circulating the story a year later, it is demoralizing for my team. As you know, we were coping with some very unusual circumstances, and it won't happen again. I'd appreciate it if you could move on."

Roxanne did not have the skill and self-control to deliver this message quietly—at least not that day, not in that moment.

How about lack of self-confidence or courage? Roxanne's group had not formally apologized to those affected by the error. The managers were discussing the incident nearly a year later because they were still angry, and the extent of the mistake had not been acknowledged. Sometimes it takes tremendous courage to apologize, especially when others are harmed by our behaviors. At the time, Roxanne and her staff had withdrawn. They became defensive as a means of deflecting attention away from their department's behavior.

Then I considered the possibility that Roxanne's behavior was the result of lack of insight. I don't think Roxanne understood how deeply her outburst offended the managers or fully comprehended the steps necessary to put the incident to bed. Instead, she continued to feed the controversy by blaming and withdrawing.

Once I looked at her behavior with a less inflammatory eye, I was also able to look at my own behavior more objectively. I too lacked skill, insight, and courage in that moment.

After her outburst, I did not know what to do. I had hit my growing edge and missed the mark. That's what we do—over and over. If we receive warm, competent feedback about errors, we learn and try again. If we make an error and the other person attacks, we reciprocate by retreating or countering his or her accusations.

After a few minutes of looking at the situation with different assumptions, I realized my queasiness was gone. When I thought about returning to Roxanne's agency for the remaining presentations, I no longer wanted to avoid her.

I learned a visceral lesson that day about the power of the subtle choices we make every time we are frustrated. Do we search for stupidity? Or do we analyze the situation in a more reflective light?

Lack of skill, insight, or courage. *Use those half-dozen words for the next few days every time you see someone who behaves rudely, defensively, or destructively.* See if you can't view their behavior as a lack of one of these three qualities. Then ask yourself, "How about me?"

Use the same words to analyze your own behavior when you make an error. Rather than disparaging ourselves for being a bad person, an idiot, or a complete bungler, we can analyze how we could approach the situation with more skill, insight, or confidence. Once thinking becomes more objective, the mood lifts, we are more motivated to change, and we are more confident that improvement is possible. Self-induced bouts of depression will become a thing of the past, as will the need to escape them by targeting someone else.

Return to the situation you would like to improve. Is there a mutual lack of skill, insight, or courage that increases the tension between you and the person with whom you're frustrated? See if you can't find a way to reframe this common human condition, help each other learn, and work toward mutual goals.

5. Negative reciprocity

Sometimes, as in the story of the president's son and the president's best friend at the print shop, the trigger for escalated conflict is simply negative reciprocity. Their mistrust for each other and their attempts to influence the president toward their faction were enough to eliminate any chance of collaboration.

While working at a hospital, "Dr. Schmitz" told me how he alienated some of his colleagues by acting on his First Assumption thinking. Dr. Schmitz worked in pediatric palliative care, which provides pain relief for children in chronic pain or near the end of their lives. The situation that troubled him the most was watching primary physicians continue treatment beyond any possibility of remission.

Prior to the class, Dr. Schmitz always assumed that the doctors were selfish and continuing treatment only because of the revenue stream. He shared this feeling with some of the nurses, and his judgments of his colleagues were, of course, passed on to the primary physicians. The primary care physicians stopped using Dr. Schmitz's services, which confirmed his belief that they were self-centered.

But during the seminar, he revisited his assumption and wondered if they were continuing treatment not because they didn't care enough, but because they cared too much and could not let go. Dr. Schmitz made a commitment: the next time he saw prolonged and unrealistic treatment, instead of talking about his colleagues behind their backs, he would reach out to them and ask what he could do to help. Up until that moment he didn't realize he had created a cycle of negative reciprocity that he could repair.

Ask yourself, "Am I and the person with whom I'm frustrated locked in negative reciprocity?" If that's a possibility, you will learn how to open the dialogue and break the cycle in the next chapter.

Summary: Five Root Causes of Workplace Tension

1. A baby in the backseat—a constraint or pressure hidden from view.
2. Poorly designed systems, work flow, or processes.
3. Performance measures that conflict.
4. Lack of skill, insight, or courage—theirs and/or yours.
5. Negative reciprocity or fear.

10

Open the Dialogue

"There are two dogs inside of every person.
The one that dominates is the one that is fed."
—Chinese parable

Typically, when we avoid reaching out to clarify our perceptions, it is because we fear we will make a moderately troubled situation worse, or, we may lack courage and skill. In this chapter, we will discuss a template to open a dialogue that is both safe and effective. Never again will you have to wonder what someone's behavior means. Rather than resorting to distorted and damaging speculations, you can ask for the other party's help to understand their actions, and you will be able to do it in a way that entices him or her to join you on a hardheaded search for solutions.

In Third Assumption, we assume that individuals *want* to be part of a high-performing group and have an intrinsic desire for achieving goals and meeting the expectations of their customers and supervisors.

Whenever tension is high or morale is languishing, it is fairly safe to assume that something—a policy, workflow, anxiety, fear, miscommunication, negative reciprocity, a personal constraint or pressure—is blocking the person's or group's ability to achieve and feel valued. In my work, I have found this to be the case vastly more often than not. As we discussed in Chapter Three, we have a drive to belong and positive workplaces are primed to fill that need.

People don't change unless they feel accepted

How can we think about others' destructive or inappropriate behavior in a way that will enhance our effectiveness? Destructive behavior is not going away, and there is plenty of it.

In order to be more effective, we do not have to take a Pollyanna approach, and think, "Isn't everyone wonderful?!" In fact, the opposite approach is more useful. Assume everyone (including you) is a nutcase. Everyone is flawed. So what is to be gained by indignation and flooding?

This is definitely *not* saying anything goes. Clearly communicated values, and enforcing methods for holding people accountable, are basic building blocks of healthy groups and organizations.

To be effective in addressing concerns let's add the concept of assertiveness to our conversation. High or low assertiveness combined with hostility or warmth results in four combinations.

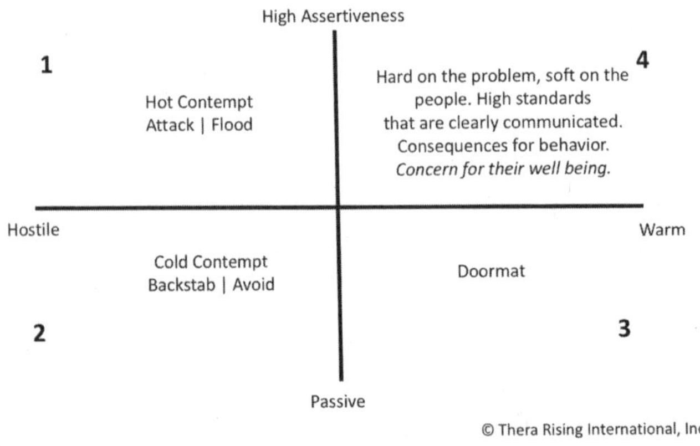

Figure 10.1. Creating positive change.

Quadrant 1: Individuals act with high hostility and high assertiveness. At Thera Rising our name for this combination is "hot contempt." In this approach, individuals are intimidating, insulting, and often flooded. In the workplace, these make up very few of the situations we address.

As I mentioned earlier, unfortunately, we often save hot contempt for the people we really love at home.

Quadrant 2: When we combine high hostility with low assertiveness, the result is "cold contempt." This is a workplace favorite. The most common behaviors in this quadrant are avoidance, backstabbing, and building adversarial factions.

Quadrant 3: The bottom right of this mental model is low assertiveness and high warmth. We call this the "Doormat" quadrant. In this approach, individuals in leadership roles (at work or home) abdicate their responsibility to shape behavior. My tongue-in-cheek example of this approach is the parent who says to his or her teenage son, "Oh, don't worry about that 'D' in algebra, honey. I failed algebra. Can you get me a beer?"

None of these approaches are effective. In the first two combinations, the other party responds with defensiveness and negative reciprocity. In the third, the supervisor or parent neglects to set and enforce healthy standards of behavior and performance.

Quadrant 4: The remaining quadrant consists of high assertiveness and warmth. This option is very effective—and it is the style that people use the least!

It's amazing to watch people gossip, stew, explode, rant, shame, stonewall, avoid, steam, make excuses, go numb, vent, roll over, use sarcasm, tease, retaliate, and suffer—reactions that take enormous physiological and emotional energy—rather than open the dialogue with warmth and clear expectations.

Asking for different behavior while treating a person with acceptance increases the odds we will maintain the relationship and work through the problem—together. If we are not experiencing connectedness, the other person is unlikely to be receptive. In the fourth quadrant, we have high standards that are clearly communicated, and there are consequences for both behaviors that are substandard and those that are optimal. However, we also convey a genuine interest in the other party's well-being, hence the warmth.

Addressing behavior in this manner has overwhelming advantages. When we give feedback with another party's interest at heart, they are tempted to listen and consider our input. The story of Rick in customized machines is a good example of how warmth made it possible to give him critical feedback.

As the following example shows, we can be warm even in situations that require dramatic corrective action.

Hard on the problem, soft on the people

I had the privilege of working with Michael, a highly skilled CEO. He has a grasp of every element of the business. He is trained in system thinking, skilled in the company's technology, is business savvy, and he has high emotional IQ.

However, Michael was stymied about one of his high-earning sales reps. Clients and board members loved Alana, but she had a reputation for being disrespectful to her peers and a bully to individuals who reported to her.

Michael told her that he kept hearing complaints about her behavior and asked her to meet with me. She agreed, and we developed a plan that we both felt was fair and constructive. Alana and I came up with a list of questions that would get at the nuances of her behavior, and, with her permission, I interviewed a variety of people across the organization. As agreed, I turned their feedback into a summary with all identifiers removed.

Alana's feedback was mixed, but most of it was harsh, and it confirmed the CEO's perceptions that she intimidated her peers and direct reports. Alana and I immediately started turning the themes of her feedback into goals. As planned, a few days later she and I met with Michael, so Alana could give him a summary of her feedback and the goals we had set.

In our meeting, Michael was a master of "hard on the problem, soft on the people." He talked with the kindness of an elder deeply concerned about Alana's future. Then, in the same gentle tone he gave her a rock-solid bottom line. No more complaints. Not one, from anyone in the organization. Michael told her if he heard one complaint, he would begin disciplinary action.

Authentic warmth wrapped in the belief that we can do better is inspirational. Alana and I met a few more times but it was hardly necessary.

She had already realized that this was the opportunity of a lifetime. She could work on the necessary changes in an atmosphere of accountability and support. I stayed in touch with Michael and Alana for the next two years, and she maintained her hard-won gains.

The Chinese gave us the "two dog" parable at the beginning of this chapter, and I often think of it when I work with individuals or teams set on destroying other people's careers. When people behave defensively or aggressively, I know the other dog—the dog of empathy and cooperation—is waiting in the wings. I can put the distressed person at ease, reduce his or her fears, and identify a way to feed the dog that wants to be appreciated and connected.

As I mentioned, we often avoid tackling tense issues head on because we fear we will make the situation worse. Opening up a conversation on a touchy or ambiguous topic takes skill and courage. In the past, if we were not prepared, we may have found that direct communication is risky, or if the other person flooded, we lacked the ability to navigate emotionally choppy waters. Rather than risk an explosive situation, we resort to withdrawal or drama-venting. However, let's look at a powerful and proven technique as an alternative.

Once you master this technique and it becomes part of your skill set, you can address sensitive issues, clear the air, and feed the dog of appreciation at the same time. It's a very empowering experience.

A Template for Success

We'll go through an overview of the five steps, and then you can sketch out a dialogue about a situation you would like to improve.

1. Affirm the relationship and mutual goal

Let's revisit several important pieces of information. John Gottman found that, 96 percent of the time, conversations end in the same energy in which they begin. Harsh setups trigger harsh endings, and conversations that open in appreciation almost always end in the same tone.

Using biofeedback data, the HeartMath Institute (*HeartMath.org*) found that when we feel and speak with appreciation, our body rhythms become coherent, and we experience a harmonization of emotional, physical, and intellectual rhythms that allow us to perform at our best. In this physiological state, we are relaxed, clear, and receptive.

Barbara Fredrickson discovered the physiological state of connectedness including the synchronization of brain waves and biochemicals between two individuals. The prerequisites of this state include a positive voice tone, eye contact, and a mutual investment in each other's well-being.

An example of connectedness: The powerful, gentle dad

I watched my friend Bob demonstrate the power of connectedness perfectly. Bob farms with his family in South Dakota, and he was one of the best parents I've ever had the pleasure of observing.

Years ago he was out in the yard with his seven-year-old son, Tommy. Bob was seated on the tractor, anxious to get to his work in the field, while Tommy was running around the yard romping about with the family dog. Bob glanced in Tommy's direction and gave him a warning about playing too closely to the auger, a dangerous, rotating conveyer belt that is used to move grain. Tommy paid no attention to his dad's instructions as he was entirely focused on his playful pal. Bob stopped the tractor, climbed down, sat on the edge of the tiller, and called his son over.

I stopped breathing. I adored Tommy, and he had disobeyed his dad. I expected Bob to yell at him, scold him harshly, or even shake him. Instead, Bob put Tommy gently on his lap, circled his arm around him protectively and asked, "Tommy, what did Daddy tell you to do?"

I was mesmerized. I had never observed anyone correct a child in such a loving fashion. I witnessed the two of them wrapped in a warm connection as Bob calmly explained the dangers of Tommy not listening. Bob had Tommy's total attention as Tommy relaxed into the curvature of his dad's arms.

Bob could not have claimed this child's rapt attention if he had flooded. We can think about flooding as static electricity that blocks the message. However, with a gentle approach, clearly based on his love for his son, Bob built a strong connection and thus increased the possibility that Tommy would respond to his warnings.

In the workplace, you can hardly sit down on the edge of the desk and invite a colleague to sit on your lap! However, you can create a climate of relaxation and acceptance by starting with a positive statement about the desire to strengthen your relationship that puts them at ease.

Remember: People need to feel accepted before they will change. As a friend and client, a vice president of IT (and a man with staggering intellect) told me, "My effectiveness skyrocketed after I realized I had the most impact when I was the least threatening."

Warmth dissolves a corporate stalemate

Alexis, a project manager at a large construction firm, gave me this example of how warmth can break through tension.

She and another project manager were in a meeting with two architects from an outside firm. The four of them were collaborating on a joint project, but they had been unable to come to an agreement about a variety of issues. The meeting was not going well, and the tension between the two groups was increasing. Unexpectedly, the president of Alexis's firm, Isaac, dropped in. Alexis told me she was thrilled and thought, "Isaac will put these architects in their place!"

However, Isaac is a master of warmth and appreciation. He greeted the visiting architects with a smile and shook their hands. He gave them a sincere compliment on a building their firm had just completed. As Isaac praised their artistry, Alexis said she could feel the tension melt on both sides of the table. Isaac expressed his delight in having great people on the team from both firms and that he couldn't wait to see their preliminary designs. He thanked them again, welcomed them to the company, shook hands, and left the room.

Alexis said that the atmosphere in the room shifted from chilly frustration to warm relaxation. Within minutes of his departure, they were on their way to resolution. Appreciation taps into the cortex where problems are solved.

This insight is priceless. When you open the dialogue, make your first statement a message that conveys your appreciation for the *relationship*. If we did not value the relationship, we would not try to fix the problem. We can learn to put those commitments, desires, and investments into words.

I helped reconnect two executives at a radio station. Ruby, the general manager, and her COO, Clyde, had not talked in more than a year, which threw their small organization into chaos. Ruby and Clyde had been close colleagues, but they both applied for the general manager position; after Ruby got the job, they stopped speaking to each other. Deeply frustrated and hurt, they each created a faction and had a cadre of loyalists. When I met with them alone, each individual was quite certain the other person was the reason for their estrangement.

The next day Clyde told me how much he missed their companionship, the laughter that had been a spontaneous byproduct of their conversations, and the ingenious radio spots they created. He thought of the much younger Ruby as his daughter and that yes, not getting the general manager job had stung, but now he wished her nothing but success.

When it was time for Clyde to sketch out how he was going to open the dialogue, his first attempt was dry and formulaic. I asked him if he would be willing to tell her what he had just told me about missing their friendship and rapport. Clyde agreed, and his energy shifted toward optimism. Reconciling with her meant a great deal to him.

The next day, when he kicked off our discussions, he acknowledged how much he missed their relationship and nonstop creativity. He spoke straight from his heart, and he was so direct and endearing that Ruby, who had been defensive and guarded, burst into tears. She too had been grieving their friendship. Although we still had several hours of work to complete, in that one-minute monologue, Clyde got us more than halfway there.

When we sincerely articulate how important someone is to us, the other person relaxes and is inclined to join us in fixing the problem. Anxiety dissipates in the face of warmth.

With a child or family member, we can say words similar to, "You're one of the most important people in my life. I want to talk to you about last night because when things aren't right between us, it troubles me throughout the day."

In the workplace we can say something similar to, "We work closely together, and it's important to me that we have a relationship based on honesty and trust. I'd like to talk with you about something that has the potential of getting in the way of our connection." Or "Unless the nursing department has a good working relationship with administration, we can't respond to clients efficiently. Would you help me with a problem that keeps tripping up customer relations?"

In the first step of opening the dialogue, we need to demonstrate that we laid down our swords; we do not intend to blame, alienate, or shame the other party. We need to make a statement about how much we value the relationship and our desire to preserve it.

How would you affirm the relationship with the person with whom you would like to speak? Why is this relationship is important to you? Like Clyde, be vulnerable. Put your intentions into words.

2. State the facts

The ability to separate fact from interpretation is a highly valuable skill. Facts don't determine how we feel; our interpretations and assumptions do.

After an event, there is a split second before interpretations and facts mingle. Being able to sort out the difference takes practice because even *what* we pay attention to is shaped by our mindset.

The following is an example of how the same event can trigger different interpretations and emotions: Imagine three people are walking down the hall at work and pass their boss, Nancy, who is walking in the opposite direction. Although Nancy is generally friendly, this particular morning she doesn't say good morning or make eye contact with anyone in the group.

When Andy interprets ambiguous behavior, he usually assumes the worst about others. He thinks, "Since she became our manager, her nose has been up in the air!" As a consequence of his thinking, Andy will be irritated and later may seek out others to validate his conclusion.

Kari's automatic interpretation is to blame herself. She thinks, "Wow, Nancy must be mad! I should not have disagreed with her in the staff meeting yesterday! Why can't I keep my mouth shut?" As a consequence of her thinking, Kari will feel anxious about their next encounter and make a commitment to stop challenging her supervisor.

Skylar is aware that interpretations are tricky. The possibilities are endless. She has learned to be curious about other individuals' behaviors. Her reaction might be, "Gee, Nancy acted like she didn't recognize us. I wonder if she has her contacts in." As a consequence of her thinking, Skylar's emotional reaction will be negligible.

Although I've listed three interpretations of one simple behavior, there are many more. Every time we interpret someone's behavior, we select from an infinite number of possibilities.

Opening the dialogue doesn't require that every assumption is correct. However, it is absolutely essential that when we make an interpretation, we know it is just that—speculation—not fact.

The wildcard of accurate interpretation: Self-confidence

Ironically, self-confidence, which is about our own state of mind, plays a role in how we interpret other people's behavior. Self-esteem is a filter. If we feel self-confident and worthy, we see others' actions in a neutral, or even positive, manner. When we feel lonely or undeserving, we view neutral behavior as additional proof of our isolation.

Whether it is about our looks, competency, ability to parent, cook, problem solve, make friends, influence, reason, sell, motivate, coach, or speak, in situations where we feel insecure, we will interpret behavior differently than in situations where we feel self-assured and competent.

The fidgeting boss

When we fail to differentiate between facts and interpretations, *we often act as if our fears are real,* and that assuredness can play a role in bringing our anxiety into reality.

Elliot went in to see his boss, AJ, with a draft of a floor plan that Elliot and his team created. As he showed AJ his work, AJ stared out the window, doodled a bit, and glanced at his laptop.

Elliot might immediately speculate about AJ's behavior: he hates the plan; he is about to leave for a doctor's appointment; he just got bad news from home; doodling helps him concentrate; he just learned that he has to cut 10 percent of his staff; and so on.

Imagine that Elliot frequently interprets AJ's behavior as dismissive and believes he is fidgeting because he dislikes the plan. Elliot rushes through his presentation and walks out of AJ's office fuming that he will never again volunteer. He tells his team that AJ is two-faced and asking for employee input is a sham. He throws the plan on a shelf.

Later, when AJ tries to follow up, Elliot brushes him off. AJ assumes that Elliot has lost interest. AJ draws the design without the team's input, muttering about how little initiative employees show these days. When Elliot learns that AJ drafted a design without input, Elliot believes his boss really did not care about the team's ideas. The next time AJ asks for input from the team, no one volunteers.

Without questioning his interpretation, Elliot never learns that AJ was distracted because just before their meeting, AJ's director had chewed him out about neglecting an important report. AJ's nervous preoccupation had nothing to do with his dislike or disapproval of the team's work.

There is a simple solution. In this step, Elliot could have checked his interpretation by stating his observations of AJ's behavior. Elliot could have said, "AJ, I noticed you have glanced at your laptop several times since I started my presentation."

If it is appropriate, use specifics. Avoid exaggeration; it will be seen as dishonest and manipulative. State your facts in such a way that the other party will agree with the accuracy and impartiality of your statement.

In the missing gaps of memory we make ourselves look a little better and the other person just a little worse. The mind fills in the most accessible data, which is usually the most negative.
—Amit Sood, MD, Mayo Clinic

If the behavior is a pattern, with a history of failed promises, start with an accurate statement that summarizes the history. An example might be, "You've made two commitments to arriving at our meetings on time, and today you were twenty minutes late." If it is a high-stakes conversation and you do not have much practice separating facts from interpretations, ask a trusted colleague or friend to review your work. What are the *facts* in the situation you are trying to improve?

3. Ask for help to understand the behavior

When we approach the third section, humility and curiosity are our best friends. We may not understand the reasons behind the other person's behavior, but we assume *something* is driving their actions.

In some schools of thought, individuals are advised to share their interpretations. For instance, Elliot could say to his boss, "I think you're glancing at your laptop and doodling because you don't like my draft." However, it is more efficient to just say, "Can you help me understand why you keep glancing at your laptop? Is everything okay?" This simple question short circuits the guessing game and leaves the door wide open for the other person to reveal his or her hidden "baby." Asking for help in understanding behavior is a respectful and neutral request for information, grounded in benign curiosity.

In general, individuals want to explain their rationale. No one wants to be judged negatively by others. Even though I often work with people who are considered unpleasant by their peers and supervisors, in three decades of conflict resolution work, I have never received a hostile response from asking, "Can you help me understand why . . .?" You may be surprised by the answer, and it might change the course of the conversation.

4. State the ideal behavior

This is a powerful and important step that we often overlook. When we are flooded or defensive, we state and restate facts and interpretations. The escape hatch from this particular dead end is to move to the future. We need to articulate what the other person or group can do to resolve the issue and restore the relationship.

You need not feel anxious about stating what you want; it is not a demand. The other person can respond with their own request or modify yours. Think of it as a starting point. Most people appreciate knowing what you want, especially if you have stated your preferences in terms of specific behavior. Avoid global statements such as, "I wish you were considerate about time" and substitute something more exact: "I wish you would call me if you're going to be more than fifteen minutes late, so I can decide if I want to wait."

For instance, after learning that AJ's focus was on other issues, Elliot could have told him how he wanted to resolve the situation. He might have suggested, "AJ, I need your reactions to the floor plan design before the team moves ahead. Can we reschedule our meeting for tomorrow morning?"

Before you open the dialogue, think about what you want from the other person. It might be as simple as setting aside time to talk, or a commitment to gather cross-functional data to work together on a problem. Do not make the mistake of the two men in the following story who argued for years without being specific about what they wanted from each other.

A specific request is a pathway back to the relationship

I was facilitating a strategic planning retreat with the management team from a chemical dependency treatment center. When a corporate client suspected an employee had a substance problem they utilized the agency for assessment, referral, and treatment.

As I gathered background information before the retreat, I learned that Joseph, the marketing director responsible for acquiring new clients, had a long-standing conflict with his peer, Mack. Mack was a recovering addict and the program director. He supervised the treatment groups and therapists. The CEO made it clear I was not hired to address this conflict. The executive team had set aside our time together to rewrite their strategic plan.

However, midway through our first morning together, this long-standing conflict erupted, and the two directors started to argue. The rest of the team pulled away from the table or turned away. Some of them walked out of the room to take phone calls or get coffee. They had heard it before and knew that once this conversation started, it took center stage.

I stood listening for several moments. Was there a way to get them unstuck within a few minutes? Or did I need to request that they table their discussion and their emotions?

As I listened, I realized that they were stating and restating facts and interpretations. Neither person was articulating what they wanted.

I interjected, "What do the two of you want from each other?"

To my amazement, instead of ticking off a list of requests, they both fell silent. This argument had been simmering for two years, yet neither person had suggested any type of solution.

Finally, Mack, the program director, said accusingly to Joseph, the director of marketing, "You don't know anything about chemical dependency.

You are selling our program and don't know squat about substance abuse or how people recover."

I prompted him again: "Mack, tell Joseph specifically what you want."

There was another pause, followed by a tentative, "I want you to go through the program as if you are a client. I want you to attend orientation and sit in on groups."

It was a pivotal moment. Everyone at the table froze.

Joseph paused for a moment and then to my amazement he said, "Okay. Actually, I've wanted to sit in on group sessions, but I was afraid it would be inappropriate."

I turned to Joseph. "Joseph, what do you want from Mack?"

There was another moment of silence. It stretched on—and on. Finally, Joseph gathered up his courage to say what he had held back for two years: "God, man, do something about your hair! When we go on sales calls, I'm embarrassed by the way you look."

In his days of using drugs, Mack hit rock bottom and remained there for a long stretch of time before he was able to maintain sobriety. Although he had been clean for many years, his days as an addict were reflected in his appearance. The clients that came to their agency were unaffected by Mark's informality. They knew Mack had walked the walk and recovered. However, when Joseph took him on sales calls to corporate offices, his unkempt hair was a definite liability.

Mack's reaction to Joseph's request was a stunner.

"Sure. I would have done it a long time ago if you asked."

I have never forgotten that moment. When we don't ask for what we want, we sacrifice the possibility of resolution.

Don't let this happen with your important issues. Again, before you open the dialogue, identify the ideal behavior you want from the other person. Make it specific and positive. What would you like the other party to do?

5. *State what you are willing to do*

You just asked someone to alter his or her behavior. Are you willing to change your behavior in return? For instance, Elliot might say to his boss, "Why don't I check in later, and we can look at your calendar?" Or the statement may be a negotiation: "If you can give me two minutes on this one detail, I can wait until later in the week for a more thorough discussion."

This statement can also be a consequence of what you will do if the other person does not change his or her behavior. If the behavior is a pattern of unkept promises, your statement may be a consequence. If you are in a position of authority, your statement may be similar to, "If this happens again, I will move to a written warning."

In the situation you want to improve, what are you willing to do to meet the other party halfway? What might be the consequence if the situation doesn't change? If at all possible stay in the energy of assertiveness and warmth.

Starting out

The first time you try this approach, use the following outline before you have the conversation. It will give you time to sort out your thinking and express those thoughts in your own words. You could open the dialogue with the situation on which you based your Cycle of Contempt.

Don't start with the worst problem in your life. Begin with more manageable situations. As your skill and confidence grows, you can tackle more complex or sensitive concerns. At some point, talking in this manner will come to you naturally, and you won't have to think it through in advance. This approach can become your best ally.

1. Affirm the relationship. "I want to talk to you because . . ." Tell the other party why you value the relationship and want to preserve it.
2. State the facts. "I noticed . . ." State the facts accurately. Be specific, and use numbers when appropriate.
3. Ask for help in understanding his or her behavior. "Can you help me understand why . . . ?" Is there a hidden constraint of pressure? A baby in the back seat?
4. State what you want. "I would prefer if you would . . ." You cannot repair this relationship by focusing on the past. What do you want in the future? Describe the ideal behavior or result.

5. State what you are willing to do. “I am willing to . . .” What are you willing to do to solve the problem? What is your part in reaching a solution? Is it necessary to impose consequences? Be specific.

11

You Can Be Successful or Self-Righteous

"As I absorbed these ideas I felt sadness, thinking about how these concepts would have changed major events in my life."

—Seminar participant

On a fairly regular basis, someone will ask me, "I understand your point, Anna, but what if someone really *is* a jerk?" and proceed to tell me about a person who seems to operate outside the realm of rational behavior. Although their stories are often amusing, the storyteller usually admits that realistically the "jerk" is a wounded, low-skill individual more deserving of compassion than contempt. Chronic hostility and cynicism is a miserable way to live.

However, the question is fair and deserves a serious answer. Is there ever a time when one should "give up" and conclude that the situation is totally the fault of the other person, it *is* permanent, and it *is* everything about them?

Let's look at a political leader who faced this decision. The individual had a multitude of reasons to treat his adversaries with aggression. Regardless, he made a decision to sacrifice his right to retaliate for an opportunity to change the trajectory of his country.

Retaliation versus reconciliation

Nelson Mandela, the former president of South Africa, wrestled with the question of effectiveness versus self-righteousness in a very public forum. In his country, from 1948 to 1990 the Dutch government ruled with institutional racism, torture, imprisonment, and the execution of thousands of black South Africans. If anyone had the right to demonize a group of individuals, Mandela did. In 1990, the world watched as he was released from prison and elected president in 1994.

In his moving autobiography, *Long Walk to Freedom*, Mandela shares how he was deeply influenced by the writings of Gandhi during the twenty-seven years he was incarcerated. He realized that blame and contempt, although justified, would not move him closer to his goal: a sustainable society. Mandela focused on changing the system, not individuals. He suspected that if he created a more healthy system, it would "feed the other dog," and his country would have an opportunity to heal.

Mandela wrote, "I know people expected me to harbor anger toward whites. But in prison, my anger toward the whites decreased and my hatred for the system grew."

Mandela let it be known that anyone who wanted to help rebuild South Africa as a nonracial democracy was welcome at the table. He broke a long-standing tradition of racial segregation, and reached out to white South Africans with an invitation to join him to create a more equitable democracy.

Mandela, together with Desmond Tutu and the former president, F. W. de Klerk, created "truth and reconciliation," a process that allowed individuals to step forward and confess to political crimes in exchange for amnesty. Under the policy, both black and white citizens had a firm deadline to confess the crimes they committed under apartheid. If they declined to take accountability, they would be criminally prosecuted.

It was an enlightened decision and allowed families on both sides of the conflict to receive reliable information about the fate of their missing loved ones. The process avoided hundreds, perhaps even thousands, of civil and criminal lawsuits—charges that would have taken decades to resolve. Truth and reconciliation allowed people to admit wrongdoing, ask for amnesty and forgiveness, and rejoin the community with an opportunity to contribute. It replaced retaliation with the possibility of reconciliation and cleared the way for a viable united future.

Videos of the tribunals were eventually broadcast in the United States, and they were wrenchingly painful to watch as perpetrators on both sides of apartheid confessed. In horrific systems, ordinary people commit heinous crimes.

However, many of Mandela and Desmond Tutu's hopes were realized. Even though they were dealing with millions of people, they showed that healthy systems can elicit healthy behavior from the same people. The country held its citizens accountable but avoided exacerbating a costly power struggle. Also, by retaining the skill base and knowledge of the previous administration and its civil servants, the newly elected government established itself with unusual speed. White and black citizens united in unprecedented cooperation. A nonracial democracy was born. There are only one or two "Mandelas" in each of our lifetimes. But these extraordinary individuals lay bare the upper limits of human potential.

Mandela chose to spend time learning about the people who had put him in jail. He studied their language, history, resentments, and fears. When the long-awaited day came and he was finally released, Mandela not only understood those who had thrown him in prison; he was able to communicate with them, find common ground with them, forgive them, and—most astonishingly—lead them.
—Madeline Albright

Partnering with the consulting company Owen, Adendorff and Associates, I had the opportunity to work in South Africa with business leaders and community activists. Siphiwi Nkabinde, Winston and Bronwyn Owen, became Thera Rising International Associates and certified to facilitate seminars based on these materials.

At one presentation a South African activist said to us, "These mental models explain a battle that goes on in my head every day. Sometimes I feel despondent that whites are never going to change, but at other moments, I see progress. Your concepts lay out these choices so simply and profoundly. I can see how my assumptions affect my outlook and effectiveness. Thank you!"

When people assure me that they know someone who deserves to be blamed—a person who qualifies as a real jerk—I respond, "If you have more evidence than Nelson Mandela I'll grant you an exception." We all make choices between matching our adversary's tone and behavior, or as Mandela did, holding individuals accountable with warmth and inviting them to join us in achieving goals of mutual gain.

Often I hit a wall when I am knee deep in a complex conflict resolution project and think, "I do not know if I can help." The feeling passes as we move beyond data collection, but usually I give myself a pep talk that consists of, "If Mandela and his associates could move 5 million people, we can move a department."

Unconsciously, you make choices between self-righteousness and effectiveness everyday. Now you can make that choice consciously.

The advantages of embracing this material

We avoid becoming emotional idiots. We will not be seen as irrational—screaming at colleagues, family members, or strangers who have a legitimate, although hidden, reason for their behavior. An automatic habit of curiosity and concern keeps us in the rational center of the brain. Remember: John Gottman found that we can't hear what the other person is saying, even if we try, once we flood and heartbeats rise above 100 beats per minute.

If you think back on the stories of transformation we covered in this book, not one of them occurred because adversaries were screaming at the other person or group. *People change because of connection, not contempt.*

Health and resiliency improve. As covered in Chapter Two, when we reduce the number of times we flood, we protect our bodies from the dangers of cardiovascular disease and the excess production of cortisol, a hormone associated with the inability to calm down, rapid aging, an impaired immune system, and damage to the cells that line the heart.

Positive reciprocity accrues. We create reciprocity with our words, tone, eye contact, and behavior. Because we are on the receiving end of the ongoing repayment of our own behavior, it makes sense to create positive reciprocity. Remember: despite what our parents said, we *are* the centers of *our* universe!

In an older but often cited study, Robert Kelley and Janet Caplan sought out top-performing engineers as identified by peers and managers. They were surprised to discover that it wasn't a superior IQ that made the difference. Employees whose performances stood out had created positive reciprocity by *cultivating relationships and friendships.* When they needed advice or input, their emails and phone calls were answered because their colleagues reciprocated their good will and the investment they had made in the other person's well-being.

People will want us on their teams. Our ability to make progress toward goals and bridge to other key players solves problems and wins friends. When we want to problem solve with another party, the skills are in our hip pockets.

Plus, positive relationships have a huge bearing on contentment. In a foundational study on happiness, relationships had the largest bearing on well-being, according to E. Diener and Martin Seligman.

We earn reputations as trustworthy, can-do leaders. Because both Cycles of Contempt and Cycles of Courage are self-fulfilling, as individuals age, patterns become more automatic and less conscious.

The blame orientation, especially as it becomes automatic, isolates us from others, and we become more cynical, ignorant, and paranoid. We are vulnerable to being be lured down dead-end roads of blame, mistrust, and negative cycles. Employees will unintentionally set us up to be suspicious of others if we tolerate their attempts to deflect personal responsibility through blame. We will buzz around in a fog of adrenaline wondering why we are surrounded by idiots, and misunderstand others' benign or even positive intentions.

In contrast, when our response to frustration and disagreement consists of curiosity and concern, we develop reputations as effective, solid, trustworthy problem solvers—the kind of person organizations develop and promote.

Love is stronger than terror because ultimately every impulse can be tracked back to our deep need for love.

—Deepak Chopra, MD

As we age: Wisdom or ignorance?

You respond to approximately thirty mini-crises or heart hassles a day, and as you have seen, all three assumptions (blame others, blame self and there's a reason) can be self-fulfilling. Imagine the impact of these thinking patterns throughout your lifetime!

With reflective rather than reflexive thinking, you will become curious about people in all walks of life. With an attitude of curiosity, you can learn about the hidden complexity of government, why hospital staffing is low, the pressures schools face, the state of highway maintenance, the constraints and pressures of media, the quirks of your neighbors, and the customs and traditions of ethnic groups. You can find out why the highways are jammed, why Millennials feel lonely, why the legislative process is slow, why the Palestinians and Israelis are mutually fearful, why your brother stopped coming to your family gatherings three years ago, and why your daughter doesn't want to play soccer anymore.

Without attack and avoid behaviors, you are in the position to learn why the driver is digging in the back seat of her car, why the boss is suddenly closing her door, why architects consistently push the envelope, and why the supervisor is missing from the shop floor.

At work you will learn about hidden influences in organizations. These understandings will allow you to identify leverage points and make your workplace more efficient and collaborative. Individuals will confide in you because they have never heard you denigrating another person or group.

The people with whom you interact trust you because you open the dialogue with respect and are willing to learn about their world. Challenges truly become opportunities to learn.

Positive energy buffers frustration. We can use it consciously to grease the wheels of human interaction. It is good for our careers, our relationships, and your heart. It shapes the quality of every interaction, every opportunity, and every challenge.

Adopting the principles of this book may be the best gift you can give yourself, your colleagues, and the people you love.

12

Create Cultures of Appreciation, Respect, Pride, and High Morale

"The space between us is where they
need to send the astronauts."
—Charlie B. Goldsmith

When I arrived at a high-tech company, Hans, the president, told me that their executive meetings dragged on, hour after unproductive hour, punctuated by outbursts of hostility and accusations. Individuals left the meeting with migraines, and often team members would refuse to talk to each other for days after they met.

By our fourth meeting, we were proceeding in a civilized tone. However, when we adjourned for lunch, I looked around the table and realized the executive team members looked pale and exhausted. I had taken away their source of energy—hostility—and hadn't replaced it. The absence of anger and outrage left a vacuum, and there was no passion or even a trace of the most basic of interactions.

When we gathered again in the conference room, I changed the afternoon agenda. I explained that we needed to move further down the continuum—away from negative energy to solidly plant the group in positive interactions before we moved on. I leaned on my relationship with Hans and asked him to be the first "receiver."

I took out a blank piece of paper and said, "I'd like you to go around the table and tell Hans one thing you respect about him as a person or one skill he brings to this table that you appreciate."

The executives stared at me as if I were mad. I sat expectantly, without apology, as if I made this request every day and, of course, they would comply. "I'll write down your comments and give them to Hans. Then we'll move to the next person. If we spend ten minutes on each person, we should be done in a little over an hour." They continued to stare at me.

I told my secret. "I know you respect each other and admire each other's dedication. Each of you shared these sentiments with me during your interview. Now you need to tell each other, or we won't have enough energy to finish the challenging analytical work that lies ahead."

Lack of recognition is the number-one reason people leave their jobs.
—Randy Sigel

They realized I was serious. Greg, the VP of engineering, turned to Hans and thanked Hans for the steady commitment he had shown in his relatively new role as president. Greg commented on Hans's business and engineering savvy, and his ability to build rapport with customers. *It was the first unadulterated statement of appreciation that had been made during a team meeting in more than a year.*

They continued around the table. Each person made a statement about Hans's talents, perspectives, and humor. As they spoke, I wrote down their remarks, and when they finished I handed them to Hans. We shifted to the next person. Again, each team member added to the list. Some individuals said one or two sentences, and some spoke paragraphs. They expanded the assignment to ninety minutes. I asked if they wanted to keep going, and they unanimously agreed. They engaged in this basic exercise for two hours. My hand cramped, and I was delighted.

Energy shifted, and shoulders softened. It was the first time I saw any of them smile. They began to build on each other's comments and acknowledged how interdependent their achievements had been.

I could see how much they had been aching to hear exactly what they were now receiving; several individuals had tears in their eyes. When we finished, everything was different.

Resentments evaporated, and transgressions were forgiven. Generosity and gratitude warmed the room. It was as if someone switched radio stations from one of silence interrupted only by criticism, to a bandwidth of humility and compassion. These simple acts actually took tremendous courage—much more than their previous accusations of wrongdoing.

For the first time I was certain that they would come through to the other side of their struggles. By creating an atmosphere of mutual respect, they were energized at a cellular level.

Within the energy of appreciation, the systemic and process problems that were the cause of their earlier hostility and hopelessness proved to be relatively easy to repair.

When organizations fail to make positive energy a habit, the daily grind of frustrations, delays, and disagreements pulls teams and groups toward negativity, pettiness, and irritability. Without positive connection, there is no fuel to sustain us.

Those individuals who lack the comfort of another human being may very well lack one of nature's most powerful antidotes to stress.
—James Lynch, MD, University of Maryland

Connections to others help us bear hard times. Even under the worst conditions—for example, combat duty—relationships make a difference in resilience. A study of World War II veterans by the United Sates Office of the Surgeon General found that combat soldiers who were members of highly bonded, cohesive groups with strong identification had fewer psychiatric breakdowns in battle. Soldiers who were lonely and isolated suffered the greatest psychological damage.

World-class appreciation

Organizations that are deeply engaged in building and maintaining cultures of appreciation seem to do so effortlessly. When positive energy reaches a critical mass, it becomes infectious and self-replicating. However, I've never been in a highly positive culture where the organization didn't consciously dedicate resources to recognizing and honoring employees, customers, and vendors.

Building lasting relationships: Ryan Companies

I have worked in hundreds of organizations, and Ryan Companies, Inc., stands out for its commitment to employees and culture. Ryan is a national leader in commercial real estate services, and when you walk in the door, massive images of their history, values, and people fill the walls. Here are some of their extraordinary practices.

- During orientation, new employees are flown to the home office from regional locations to learn about the founding of the company, business operations, meet company leadership, and to hear stories that bring Ryan values to life.
- A nine-month training program for emerging leaders includes cross-functional teams and real-time projects. High-potential employees are challenged with finding solutions and developing innovative ideas to improve efficiency and quality. Through research and teamwork, each team presents their results to company leadership, and the majority of the ideas are implemented. The program is transformational for participants as their visibility and confidence soars.
- To minimize compartmentalization, the home office caters lunches every two weeks, and employees sit with a colleague with whom they haven't had much contact.
- Twice a year each region convenes for all-employee meetings to discuss financial updates, hear strategic benchmarks, and

ask questions. Every employee from the CEO to construction workers crowd into the room.

- The company marked their eightieth year of business by hosting a three-day, company-wide celebration and learning event.
- Ryan encourages 5 percent of work time to be spent volunteering in community social service agencies and pitching in during natural disasters. This spirit of altruism spreads between colleagues. Employees rally around coworkers by wearing colors that bring awareness of cancers being fought by colleagues, and collecting food and staples for families in distress.
- One example that touched me deeply: A Ryan project manager died without warning two years after he left Ryan. In an extraordinary act of camaraderie and kindness, a few weeks after his funeral, a Ryan employee called his widow and asked how they could help. The widow shared that she was surrounded by her husband's unfinished household repairs. The following weekend a dozen employees went to the former employee's home and completed several projects, including pouring new concrete steps.
- Recognition of employees is the centerpiece of Ryan celebrations. Every November, the 1,300 Ryan employees begin peer nominations for the next recipient of the Jim Ryan Award. Criteria for nominations include "honesty and integrity," "exceptional dedication and service," "keen loyalty and pride," and "a willingness to assist and help others." Past recipients of the award review the peer nominations and make the final choice. Family members are sworn to secrecy and invited to participate in the celebration. Along with company-wide recognition, the recipient is awarded a $5,000 gift to the *charity of their choice.*

Culture trumps strategy every time.
—Pat Ryan, Chairman of the Board, Ryan Companies

In large and small ways, this company understands the importance of its employees and sharing the rewards of their success through recognition and inclusion.

Impressions of warmth and competence account for 90 percent of the impact we make on others according to C. Porath and A. Gerbasi. In a 2014 article, they reported that people were almost 60 percent more willing to share information from civil individuals. They found that the one behavior of leaders that had the single most powerful effect on employees was respect.

Best practices

Much has been written on acknowledging and recognizing employees. Although these books are rich in ideas, I recommend you base your practices of appreciation on your own experiences. When have you felt truly honored and appreciated at work? When did you feel that recognition programs were superficial, or even insulting? What were the ingredients? What makes appreciation special and meaningful, or hollow?

I suggest that you seek input from employees. Feedback can be collected in focus groups, interviews, or surveys. If you create a standing group that is dedicated to recognition, include upper management, middle employees, and frontline employees, and rotate the positions every year. As a result, you'll get fresh ideas from a cross-section of the organization, and more individuals will have a stake in the process.

Another option is to create or open channels of internal and external customer feedback. Encourage employees to interview between three to five key customers a year to learn how their work affects others and what creates satisfaction from the customer's perspective.

Love is an infinite victory.
—Yogi Tea

Some organizations wisely benchmark other company's recognition practices. I'm always asking my clients to tell me about moments when they've felt honored or truly appreciated at work. Following is a partial list of recent answers.

1. After attending a seminar on this material, a customer service group started an "anti-flooding" team to identify and eliminate sources of frustration and aggravation.
2. Not all gestures need be elaborate or expensive. One successful tax accountant presents a chocolate bar when her clients come in to sign their taxes. The bar is molded with the IRS 1040 form and the wrapper reads, "Take a bite out of taxes!" Funny, memorable, and an inexpensive way to show appreciation at the conclusion of a process that is rarely uplifting, clients leave with a smile.
3. A CEO in Minneapolis sends a handwritten birthday card to every employee. While I was working there, I heard about this practice spontaneously from at least ten different employees. He also has a practice of granting loans to long-term employees. Their human resource person told me no one has ever reneged on a loan.
4. Many companies allow employees to donate vacation or sick time to employees during a crisis. At one company, an employee suffered a stroke a year from retirement, and employees voluntarily paid his health and pension contributions so their colleague could retire with a full pension.
5. In one high-appreciation culture in England, the managing director (CEO) excused himself from a conversation with a member of Parliament to open the hallway door for the janitor who was carrying a cumbersome box. The incident

had occurred years before I arrived. However, his behavior clearly made a lasting impression. During two days I was onsite, I heard the story from four different employees.

6. A client spoke of a practice that meant a lot to employees. They have three call centers, but only one of them offers twenty-four-hour service. When the twenty-four-hour location is closed for maintenance, the overnight calls are routed to a sister site. Folks at the receiving locations are not thrilled about working overnight, so they turn it in to a party. The manager brings in espresso machines and makes lattes and mochas throughout the night, and takes a moment to visit with each of the 200 employees and thanks them as he delivers a beverage to their desks.

7. I consulted with a company that was concerned when the operations division at one site reported significantly lower employee satisfaction scores than the other divisions. As part of our project, we brainstormed with employees how *they* wanted to be recognized and used a multiple voting technique to identify their top three choices—all of which management agreed to. The leaders were astonished! No one anticipated the preferences of the operators. The winning ideas included 1) being allowed to work overtime Monday through Thursday, so they could leave at noon on Friday prior to holiday weekends; 2) sponsoring barbeque cook offs in the summer (employees made it clear they didn't want it catered; they wanted to do it themselves, and show off their best and most extreme sauces); and 3) requesting a visit to a customer site in small groups once a year to see the impact of their work. The leadership team of the division was simultaneously floored and buoyed by what employees collectively agreed was meaningful to them.

These practices are fun and inspiring to read. However, the best rituals of appreciation are unique to the culture and nature of your organization. Rituals are meaningful when they are consistent with the values and identity of the organization, and the impact your organization has on both internal and external customers and clients.

You can trust that your colleagues want to be connected and that they yearn for recognition of their contributions. For many individuals this is what gives their work, and lives, meaning. Find ways to survey their needs and dreams, and turn them into reality. Don't be afraid to ask, and ask again.

Epilogue: Transforming the Enemy

"If you keep a green bough in your heart,
the singing bird will come."
—Proverb

In *The Structure of Scientific Revolution,* Thomas Kuhn concluded that even scientists don't see data that is inconsistent with their beliefs. The physicist Max Planck wrote, "A new scientific truth does not triumph by convincing its opponents and making them see the light, but rather because its opponents eventually die and a new generation grows up that is familiar with it."

If scientists, who ground their work on precision and objectivity, struggle to see opposing data, imagine how easy it is for nonscientists to convince themselves that their conclusions are accurate and rational.

Our desires shape the data to which we pay attention. If we decide someone is a jerk, our brains cooperate and filter out facts that disagree with our conclusion. We selectively screen memories and perceptions that support our beliefs about someone, or something, even as we assure ourselves that we are being objective.

The following story is an illuminating example of how my unconscious choice to search for stupidity rather than looking for underlying reasons made me part of a problem that was close to my heart. Although this story is from my personal life, the lessons I learned have profoundly shaped my work.

Years ago, during the second week of my new job in South Dakota, I noticed a woman standing discreetly in the corner of a crowded elevator. She had striking blond hair falling to her waist, and even though it was a relatively formal workplace, she had a noticeable hole in her sweater. I was struck by the contrast of her natural beauty and the blemish in her clothing.

A few weeks later, colleagues introduced us, and we discovered a mutual love of books, music, and conversation. As I got to know Jenny, I realized that her appearance reflected her personality quite accurately. She was witty, accomplished, and a bit of a rebel. There was always a button missing, a hem slightly undone, or sleeves hanging below her wrists.

Central South Dakota, with its low population and scarce amenities, is a do-it-yourself state. If you don't create your own amusement, you are not entertained. Hence, after Jenny and I met, we quickly became adventurous friends who cooked up all kinds of interesting things to do. We frequently drove out to the river to watch the moonrise, took midnight swims in the summer, and snowshoed our way to winter picnics amidst the state's untamed beauty.

Years later Jenny moved east to continue her training as a nurse practitioner, and I returned to Minnesota to enter graduate school. We stayed connected through phone calls and visits.

A few years after her move, her calls included breathy, excited updates about Stan, the new love in her life. Despite an intense attraction at the onset of their relationship, by the third year Jenny began to vacillate between happiness and despair. Periods of intimacy were punctuated with weeks of estrangement and tears. After one of their painful breakups, Jenny called me with a sobering announcement: "I'm pregnant."

I felt a rush of mixed emotions thinking about what a fun-loving and devoted mother she would be, and simultaneously knowing she would struggle, far from family and friends, to create financial stability and a network of emotional support.

After Jenny told Stan she was pregnant, they made one last attempt to reconcile, but their reconnection dissolved within weeks. Jenny, with her endearing qualities of pride and defiance, was determined to raise her child alone. Several months later, she home-birthed a beautiful, healthy daughter named Alicia.

During the months that followed, Jenny and her geographically distant but close-knit circle of friends struggled with grief and bewilderment over the missing and enigmatic father. We hoped that Stan would reenter her life, or Jenny would find a partner who would help raise Alicia as his daughter. However, the years passed, Alicia grew into a precocious youngster, and we continued to hear nothing from Stan. The magical stepfather never materialized.

Through mutual friends we learned that Stan had moved across the state and married a woman with two children. Although he was aware of Alicia's birth and had returned multiple times to the town where Alicia lived, he made no attempts to see his daughter.

When Alicia was present, Jenny and I stayed matter-of-fact about Stan's absence. But privately, our dislike for him became a source of camaraderie. Our anger, like all contempt, had a subtle payoff. No matter what strains developed in the relationship between Jenny and I, there was always a handy source of agreement; we could instantly connect and be energized by focusing on our mutual disdain of Stan.

However, when Alicia turned seven, she began reacting to Stan's absence. She became increasingly preoccupied and inconsolable about her absent father and began crying herself to sleep. She was restless and became disruptive at school. It was obvious that she needed to connect with her father or find closure to the possibility that he would never be part of her life.

During a visit, Jenny got a babysitter for Alicia, and she and I went out for a quiet meal. The conversation turned to the well-worn subject of Stan's absence. However, with Alicia's growing unhappiness weighing heavily on my mind, something shifted, and a sense of discomfort grew. I began listening to our conversation with a detached perspective and realized that our images of Stan were distorted by our contempt.

We were deep in First Assumption thinking. Jenny and I framed the situation as if the whole problem was Stan's character, as if he was totally useless, and he would never change.

In reality, I wasn't behaving well either. For the first time I realized that *my* thinking was part of the problem. By striving to be supportive of my precious friend, I had unintentionally made *Alicia's* struggle more difficult.

In that moment I realized Alicia wasn't suffering just because of her father's behavior, but she was paying a price for my behavior too. My self-righteousness had become part of our inability to solve the problem.

I put down my fork, surprised by what I was about to say. "Jenny, we have to stop talking about Stan as if he's the enemy. We have to reach out to him. He needs to know how important he is to Alicia. I am willing to find him and bring him up to speed on what's going on.

There was dead silence. Jenny looked as if she was struggling to understand what I had just said. "We have to tell him how important he is. We have to at least try."

Jenny was taken aback by my sudden shift and hesitated. "Let me think about it." The next day, during a long drive back to Minnesota, I had hours to mull over what had happened and hold myself accountable. I realized that my self-righteous indignation had kept me from seeing Stan with curiosity. Because of my disappointment in his behavior, he became an easy target of my wrath. I had unconsciously given my brain the command, "Search for stupidity! Stan is a jerk!" and my brain had responded. I swept over the complex story of their relationship with disdain toward the missing person.

I saw how the allure of self-righteousness energy had also boxed us in, leaving no possibility of resolution.

During the drive, I tried a mental exercise. I came up with as many answers as I could to the question, "Why would a reasonable person do what Stan has done? *Why* would he withdraw?"

I had given my brain a totally different command: "Help me understand," and for the first time in seven years, I analyzed the situation using Third Assumption.

What was Stan's hidden constraint or pressure? Could he think Alicia was better off without him? Maybe he felt awkward and didn't know how to initiate a connection. Perhaps when Stan discovered Jenny was pregnant he asked her to put the baby up for adoption, and she had refused. Perhaps, overwhelmed with anger and fear, Jenny had told him she never wanted to see him again.

Maybe he felt inadequate and ashamed, and thought Alicia wanted nothing to do with him. Perhaps he was ill or chemically dependent. Possibly his new wife was putting pressure on him to leave his daughter in his past. Maybe he thought his lack of involvement would make it more likely Jenny would find a partner. Maybe Stan didn't want to be a father at that moment in time and felt the pregnancy had been intentional and thus he felt justified in his withdrawal and lack of support. Maybe he felt trapped and responded by refusing to take responsibility.

I realized these thoughts were speculations, but even contemplating them was breathtaking. I had allowed my behavior to be driven by inflammatory and adversarial assumptions. When I wanted to see Stan as the "bad guy," I overlooked important facts, and my mind created an image of him that fit my intention to make him the scapegoat.

When I examined the situation without judgment, and tried to understand him instead, my hostility toward him dissolved and I saw his behavior in a different light. I considered facts that I had previously ignored. Similar to scientists blinded by the limitations of their existing paradigm, my mind limited the data to support my conclusion.

I still wanted Stan to take responsibility for his daughter, but now, without the burden of contempt, I could think of a multitude of reasons for why he might have withdrawn. In addition, I saw an endless number of ways to reach out to him and open the dialogue.

Several days later, Jenny called and read me a letter she had written to the absentee father. She had written poignantly about Alicia's longing for him and prepared a small parcel with recent photos of Alicia and stories she had written in school.

During this pivotal conversation Jenny and I cried, laughed, and supported each other in the importance, and unfamiliarity, of this new direction. Then we collectively held our breaths, not daring to expect much, but hoping for some kind of reaction.

Stan responded. Strained phone calls between Stan and Jenny eventually evolved into plans for a meeting. Several weeks later, we sat down for Thanksgiving dinner in my home. Jenny and I were dizzy with the reality that he was really there. We couldn't believe it was happening.

Alicia sized up her dad and vacillated between, "Isn't he cool?" and "Can we go now?" Despite our useless negative speculation about Alicia's father, there he was—looking older, a bit fragile, with a slight tremor in his hands and a catch in his voice. At our first meeting Stan didn't offer any explanation for his absence, and we didn't ask. Bless him—it was enough that he was there.

That evening, Alicia began a cycle of feelings that ran through happy, ambiguous, sad, mad, delighted, the desire to please him, and the need to reject him, that would take many years to run its course.

Like her mother, Alicia is now a beautiful, accomplished young woman. Her father has remained an active, loving presence in her life and played a significant role in contributing to her college expenses.

In addition to healing my heart about Alicia's well-being, I learned a lot from my thinking and have often reflected on the power of assumptions to create reality. I suspect many of us get caught in the same self-fulfilling dilemma.

In many ways the experience with Alicia's father helped solidify the principles of my work, including:

- When we tap the energy of contempt, we often demonize a hurting, insecure person. We sever relationships and lose the possibility of resolution.
- If we want to believe that someone is a fool, our minds will make it so.
- If we search to understand why a person is behaving in a particular manner, different data becomes available.
- Self-righteous indignation makes it more likely, not less, that the other person will behave in an irresponsible manner.
- Being hard on the problem but soft on the people appeals to our higher angels and increases our chances of success.
- Being needed matters.
- Holding others accountable in a climate of warmth is infinitely more effective than avoidance and denigration.
- One person can take the first step that breaks a Cycle of Contempt.
- It is never too late.

Acknowledgments

The publishing team at Red Wheel/Career Press: Michael Pye, Kathryn Sky-Peck, Bonni Hamilton, Laurie Kelly and Jane Hagaman; Jim Anderl of Vistage; the kind feedback of Andy Dahl, Marie Burgeson and Erin Bouchard; the support of Mary Butler—a little bird with jeweled heart; Danielle Martin; Rod Sando; Joyce Quarnstrom; Gordy Vande-Voorde; Sandra Johnson; Theresa Rotter; Magda Waer; Drea Zigarmi; Susan Fowler; Pat Zigrami; Brian Lassiter and Jennifer Burmeister of Performance Excellence Network; Donna Corbo; Fran Van Bockel; Erin O'Hara Myer and Wendy Madsen of Ryan Companies; John Fechter and Gary Floss of the School of Engineering, University of St. Thomas; Greg Lee and Meg Donahue of Carl Zeiss; George Whelock; Kathie Kosharek; Patrick Logelin; Deondra Dee Avery; Sheila Moore; Penni Perri; Karen Borre; Charlotte Mardell; Margaret Kloster; Lorry Alexander; Women on Fire; the Golden Lake book club; the writing sanctuary at Naniboujou Lodge; and my large, irreverent, and precious Greek family.

Associates of Thera Rising International, Inc.

Finland: Tapio Siren, MS

The UK: Paul Norrington, BSc

South Africa: Siphiwe Nkabinde, Diploma in Industrial Relations, Certificate in Methodist Local Preachers; Bronwyn Owen, BA; and Winston Owen, BA, Hons

New Hampshire: Elizabeth Labonte, MS; and Katie Stanley, LCMHC

Michigan: Leslie Fiorenzo, MA; Steve Gainey, MA, Licensed Psychologist; and Pam Wyess, MSA

Nevada: Dave Mather, EdD

New York: Richard Demers, LMHC, CEAP, SPHR

Greater Minnesota: Aurea Osgood, PhD; Lori Mjoen; Sandy Reed; Lori Reed, MBA; Ann MacDonald, MA; Kyle Heyesen, MSW; Crystal Hanson, MA; and Betty Strehlow, PhD

Twin Cities: Julie Sampson, BA; Nancy Jannik, PhD; Ben Martin, BA; Shawn Judge, BA; Kalli Matsuhashi, MA, Licensed Psychologist; Pam Nelson, PCC, CPCC; Lisa Habisch, SPHR, SWP; Sue EckMaahs; Donna Corbo; and Karen Borre, BA

Bibliography

Agrawal, Rahul, and Fernando Gomez-Pinilla. "Metabolic Syndrome in the Brain: Deficiency in Omega-3 Fatty Acid Exacerbates Dysfunctions in Insulin Receptor Signalling and Cognition." *The Journal of Physiology* 590, no. 10 (2012): 2485–2500.

Albrecht, G. "Chronic Environmental Change: Emerging 'Psychoterratic' Symptoms." In *Climate Change and Human Well-Being: Global Challenges and Opportunities,* edited by I. Weissbecker, 43–56. New York: Springer, 2011.

Albright, Madeleine. *Fascism: A Warning.* New York: HarperCollins, 2018.

American Automobile Association (AAA). *Prevalence of Self-Reported Aggressive Driving Behavior: United States, 2014.* Washington, DC: AAA Foundation for Traffic Safety, July 2016.

American Psychiatric Association. *Public Opinion Poll in 2018 Annual Meeting. www.psychiatry.org.*

Aronson, Elliot. "Reducing Hostility and Building Compassion." In *The Social Psychology of Good and Evil,* second edition, edited by Arthur G. Miller. New York: The Guilford Press, 2004.

Biette-Timmons, Nora. "Guns During Road Rage Incidents." *The Trace Newsletter,* August 10, 2017.

Callahan, David. *The Cheating Culture: Why More Americans Are Doing Wrong to Get Ahead.* San Diego: Harcourt, 2004.

Bushman, Brad J. "Does Venting Anger Feed or Extinguish the Flame? Catharsis, Rumination, Distraction, Anger, and Aggressive Responding." *Personality and Social Psychology Bulletin* 28, no. 6 (June 2002): 724–731.

Cassino, Dan, and Krista Jenkins. "Beliefs About Sandy Hook Cover-Up, Coming Revolution Underlie Divide on Gun Control." *Fairleigh Dickinson University* PublicMind Poll, 2013. *http://publicmind.fdu.edu.*

Centers for Disease Control and Prevention. "Leading Causes of Death Reports, 1981-2016." February 2017. *cdc.gov.*

Childre, Doc, and Howard Martin. *The HeartMath Solution.* New York: HarperCollins, 1999.

Cigna U.S. *Loneliness Index: Survey of 20,000 Americans Examining Behaviors Driving Loneliness in the United States.* May 2018.

Crocker, Jennifer. "The Worthy Self." Minneapolis: Cortex Continuing Education Course, 2003.

Diener, Ed, and Martin E. P. Seligman. "Very Happy People." *Pyschological Science* 13, no 1 (January 2002): 81–84.

Eckman, Paul. *Emotions Revealed: Recognizing Faces and Feelings to Improve Communication and Emotional Life.* Second edition. New York: Owl Books, 2007.

Eisenberger, Naomi. "Why Rejection Hurts." In *Future Science: Essays from the Cutting Edge,* edited by Max Brockman, 170–183. New York: Vintage, 2011.

Foulk, Trevor, Andrew Woolum, and Amir Ere. "Catching Rudeness Is Like Catching a Cold: The Contagion Effects of Low-Intensity Negative Behaviors." *Journal of Applied Psychology* 101, no. 1 (2016): 50–67.

Fredrickson, Barbara L. *Love 2.0—Creating Happiness and Health in Moments of Connection.* New York: Penguin, 2013.

Fritze, J., G. A. Blashki, S. Burke, and J. Wiseman. "Hope, Despair and Transformation: Climate Change and the Promotion of Mental Health and Well-Being." *International Journal of Mental Health Systems* 2 (2008): 13.

Gallup Inc. "Worry About Hunger, Homelessness Up for Lower-Income in U.S." Jeffrey M. Jones. March 30, 2017.

———. "World Took a Negative Turn in 2017." Julie Ray. September 2018.

Goodwin, A., L. Thomas, B. Kirley, W. Hall, N. O'Brien, and K. Hill. "Countermeasures That Work: A Highway Safety Guide for State Highway Safety Office, 8th Edition." Washington, DC: National Highway Traffic Safety Administration. 2015 Report No. DOT HS 812 202.

Gottman, John M. *The Seven Principles for Making Marriage Work*. New York: Crown Publishers, 1999.

Hanson, Rick. *Hardwiring Happiness: The New Brain Science of Contentment, Calm, and Confidence*. New York: Harmony Books, 2013.

Holt-Lunstad, Julianne, Timothy B. Smith, M. Baker, T. Harris, and D. Harris. "Loneliness and Social Isolation as Risk Factors for Mortality: A Meta-Analytic Review." *Perspectives of Psychological Science* 10, no. 2 (2015): 227–2337.

Johnson, Sue. *Hold Me Tight: Seven Conversations for a Lifetime of Love*. New York: Little, Brown, 2008.

Karpman, Michael, Stephen Zuckerman, and Dulce Gonzalez. "The Well-Being and Basic Needs Survey." Urban Institute. August 2018.

Kelley, Robert and Janet Caplan. "How Bell Labs Create Star Performers." *Harvard Business Review*. 1993. *hbr.org*.

Kohn, Alfie. *No Contest: The Case Against Competition*. New York: Houghton Mifflin, 1992.

Kuhn, Thomas. *The Structure of Scientific Revolution: 50th Anniversary Edition*. Fourth edition. Chicago: University of Chicago Press, 2012.

Mandela, Nelson. *Long Walk to Freedom*. New York: Little, Brown, 1994.

National Institute of Mental Health. *Statistics on Any Disorder*. November 2017. *www.nimh.nih.gov*.

Neff, Kristin. *Self-Compassion: Stop Beating Yourself Up and Leave Insecurity Behind*. New York: HarperCollins, 2011.

Pew Research Center report 2016. "What the World thinks About Climate Change." *www.pewresearch.org*.

Porath, Christine. *Mastering Civility: A Manifesto for the Workplace*. New York: Grand Central Publishing, 2016.

Porath, Christine, and Alexandra Gerbasi. "Does Civility Pay?" *Organizational Dynamics* 44 (2015): 281–286.

Porath, Christine, and Christine Pearson. "The Price of Incivility." *Harvard Business Review*. January-February 2013. *https://hbr.org.*

Porath, Christine, Deborah MacInnis, and Valerie Folkes. "Witnessing Incivility Among Employees: Effects on Consumer Anger and Negative Inferences About Companies." *Journal of Consumer Research* 37, no. 2 (2010): 292–303.

Ranson, M. "Crime, Weather and Climate Change." *Harvard Kennedy School M-RCBG Associate Working Paper Series*, no. 8 (2012). doi:10.2139/ssrn.2111377.

Riskin, Arieh, Amir Erez, Trevor A. Foulk, Amir Kugelman, Ayala Gover, Irit Shoris, Kinneret S. Riskine, and Peter A. Bamberger. "The Impact of Rudeness on Medical Team Performance: A Randomized Trial." *Pediatrics* 136, no. 3 (2015) 487–495.

Robertson, Katie. "Six Things We Learned from Young Adults Experiencing Gun Violence in Chicago." *Urban Institute Newsletter.* October 17, 2018.

Saslow, Eli. *Rising Out of Hatred: The Awakening of a Former White Nationalist.* New York: Double Day, 2014.

Schwartz, C., J. B. Meisenhelder, Y. Ma, and G. Reed. "Altruistic Social Interest Behaviors Are Associated with Better Mental Health." *Psychosomatic Medicine* 65, no. 5 (Sept.-Oct. 2003): 778–785.

Sood, Amit. *The Mayo Clinic Guide to Stress-Free Living.* Philadelphia: Da Capo Press, 2013.

———. *The Mayo Clinic Handbook for Happiness*. Philadelphia: Da Capo Press, 2015.

Southern Poverty Law Center. "Hate Groups: State Totals Map." Accessed October 2018. *www.splcenter.org.*

Spiegel, David, Helena C. Kraemer, Joan R. Bloom, and Ellen Gottheil. "Effect of Psychosocial Treatment on Survival of Patients with Metastatic Cancer." *The Lancet* 334, no. 8668 (1989): 888–891.

Stroebel, Charles F. *QR: The Quieting Reflex.* New York: Berkley Books. 1985.

Taylor, Jill Bolte. *My Stroke of Insight: A Brain Scientist's Personal Journey.* New York: Viking/Penguin, 2008.

Tavris, Carol. *Anger: The Misunderstood Emotion.* New York: Touch-Stone Books/Simon & Schuster, 1989.

Tedeschi, Richard, and L. Calhoun. "Posttraumatic Growth: Conceptual Foundation and Empirical Evidence." *Psychological Inquiry* 15 (2004):1–18.

Thorne, Deborah, Pamela Foohey, Robert M. Lawless, and Katherine M. Porter. "Graying of U.S. Bankruptcy: Fallout from Life in a Risk Society." *Social Science Research Network.* August 2018. *ssrn.com.*

Tutu, Desmond, Dalai Lama, and Douglas Abrams. *The Book of Joy.* New York: Avery, 2016.

Twenge, Jean M. "The Evidence for Generation Me and Against Generation We."

Society for Emerging Adulthood and *SAGE Publications* 1, no.1 (2013): 11–16.

United Nations. "Report of the Special Rapporteur on Extreme Poverty and Human Rights on his Mission to the United States of America." Special Rapporteur: Phillip Alston. (May 4, 2018): A/HRC/38/33/Add.1.

Watterson, Kathryn. *Not by the Sword: How a Cantor and His Family Transformed a Klansman.* Boston: Northeastern University Press, 2000.

World Health Organization report 2018. "800,000 People Kill Themselves Every Year, What Can We Do?" *www.who.int.*

Williams, Ray. "Workplace Bullying: Norths America's Silent Epidemic." Workplace Bullying Institute Blog. May 4, 2011. *www.workplacebullying.org.*

Williams, Redford. *The Trusting Heart: Great News About Type A Behavior.* New York Times Books, 1989.

Williams, Redford, and Virginia Williams. *Anger Kills.* New York: Harper Perennial, 1993.

Index

About the Author

Anna Maravelas, president of Thera Rising International and Psychologist Emeritus, MA, has resolved more than 300 workplace conflicts. She has a graduate degree in Psychology with additional training in system thinking and process mapping. Anna studied conflict resolution at Harvard Law School's Negotiation Project. Every year, Anna and her Associates teach thousands of leaders, employees, and faculty how to preempt and resolve escalated conflict and mistrust. In addition to delivering keynotes and seminars, Maravelas teaches her advanced strategies in conflict resolution to human resource and organization development professionals. Her work has been featured on numerous business radio shows and in print media including *Oprah Magazine, Harvard Management Update,* and MSNBC. The *New York Times* named her "The best source on workplace tension and mistrust." She resides in the Twin Cities of Minnesota.

You can further your skills:

- Go to our website to find a Thera Rising Associate in your area, and to learn about upcoming events and new products.
- Sign up for our blog at ConflictSavvy.net
- Invite us to facilitate a presentation at your workplace or conference
- Contact us about a conflict resolution project
- Complete train the trainer for becoming a Thera Rising Associate
- Participate in Thera Rising's "Certificate Program in Workplace Conflict Resolution"

Remember to feed the right dog, first in yourself and then out in a world that desperately needs to discover what is covered in these pages.

info@TheraRising.com | *www.TheraRising.com* | Thera (Greek): To heal